UNDERSTANDING AND LOVING A PERSON WITH

ATTENTION DEFICIT DISORDER

UNDERSTANDING AND LOVING A PERSON WITH

ATTENTION DEFICIT DISORDER

*Biblical and Practical Wisdom
to Build Empathy, Preserve Boundaries,
and Show Compassion*

STEPHEN ARTERBURN, M.Ed.
AND TIMOTHY SMITH, M.Ed.

David C Cook®
transforming lives together

UNDERSTANDING AND LOVING A PERSON
WITH ATTENTION DEFICIT DISORDER
Published by David C Cook
4050 Lee Vance Drive
Colorado Springs, CO 80918 U.S.A.

David C Cook U.K., Kingsway Communications
Eastbourne, East Sussex BN23 6NT, England

The graphic circle C logo is a registered trademark of David C Cook.

The website addresses recommended throughout this book are offered as a
resource to you. These websites are not intended in any way to be or imply an
endorsement on the part of David C Cook, nor do we vouch for their content.

Details in some stories have been changed to protect the identities of the persons involved.

Unless otherwise noted, all Scripture quotations are taken from the Holy Bible,
NEW INTERNATIONAL VERSION®, NIV®. Copyright © 1973, 2011 by
Biblica, Inc.® Used by permission. All rights reserved worldwide. NEW INTER-
NATIONAL VERSION® and NIV® are registered trademarks of Biblica, Inc. Use
of either trademark for the offering of goods or services requires the prior written
consent of Biblica, Inc. Scripture quotations marked ESV are taken from the ESV®
Bible (The Holy Bible, English Standard Version®), copyright © 2001 by Crossway,
a publishing ministry of Good News Publishers. Used by permission. All rights
reserved. The author has added italics to Scripture quotations for emphasis.

LCCN 2017935674
ISBN 978-1-4347-1055-0
eISBN 978-1-4347-1234-9

The Author is represented by and this book is published in association with the
literary agency of WordServe Literary Group, Ltd., www.wordserveliterary.com.

Cover Design: Amy Konyndyk
Cover Photo: Getty Images

Printed in the United States of America
First Edition 2017

1 2 3 4 5 6 7 8 9 10

072817

Contents

Introduction

You are holding in your hand a dream I have had for a very long time. The entire Arterburn Wellness Series fulfills a vision and desire to help those who need an extra dose of compassion and understanding. If you're like the thousands I have had the privilege of talking with over the years as the host of *New Life Live!*, you have likely experienced greater frustration than you ever thought possible, along with despair, hopelessness, and even moments when you thought you just might lose it altogether.

Attention deficit disorder (ADD) and attention deficit hyperactivity disorder (ADHD) are real. Those who know me well know that I've had ADD my entire adult life. That doesn't make me bad or hard to handle; it just means my attention span can put a crimp in some peoples' style.[1]

In my experience, people who have a loved one with ADD often struggle in the dark. Many of the standard methods that are supposed to help just make matters worse, and life seems darker with each failed attempt.

You might have wanted to give up at some point. Perhaps you already have. That's where this book comes in.

First of all, I want this to help you. I hope that after you read this short book on understanding and loving someone with ADD, your long suffering will make sense, and the path forward will be freedom from all the damage that can be done to a relationship with ADD at the center. The liberty I want for you is not found in throwing up your hands and giving up. No matter where you are in your relationship with someone who is struggling, I want you to be free from shame and self-condemnation. Few have the formal training to relate to someone who seems so distracted and disorganized. I want you to understand why you sometimes react the way you do, and I want you to develop new responses that leave you feeling better—responses that might help build a relationship (or heal from the pain of an unsalvageable one).

I wish everyone I've known had read this book by Tim Smith, a friend, family coach, and adult with ADD … like me. They would have understood their frustrations, and their sometimes abrupt reactions. It would have helped people like me. If you have ADD, I hope you feel understood as you read this book. Those of us with ADD have a quite predictable (though complicated) brain that is sometimes unable to focus and attend to the details that make for a healthy relationship. It stands to reason that you are more likely to stay with a person with ADD—and enjoy staying with them—if you understand why they do the things they do … and what you can do to help.

Please read this book with an open mind and heart. Realize that no two cases of ADD or ADHD are alike. Not every person who is unfocused or hyperactive can be fully categorized; some are light, some are extreme. But if you apply the following principals and concepts to your unique situation, this book can change everything.

I hope you learn that there is no reason to deal with this alone. There is help and support available. I have severe ADD and a bit of Asperger's as well. When my wife attended an Asperger's support group, she found tremendous relief. Just knowing she wasn't crazy—that others had dealt with the same issues—gave her great hope. I think you would find the same in a group, and I know you will find hope in this little book.

—Stephen Arterburn

CHAPTER ONE

Wasted Time

The K-cup coffee maker hissed as it brewed an extra-large serving into a disposal cup. The digital clock read 6:17 a.m. Morning network news stridently reported the chaos du jour as Gabriela dried her hair in the kitchen. With her head bent over and her hair hanging down, she caught a glimpse of the time.

"Oh, crud, I'm late!"

She clicked the dryer off, popped a lid onto her coffee cup, grabbed her backpack, and scurried to grab a piece of toast from the toaster.

"Oh, no! I forgot to push it down!" Gabriella would often talk to herself in an attempt to organize her mind. *I'm gonna be late for work!*

She snatched a protein bar to eat on the way. She was a college professor and department head, and today she was presenting a key proposal to her colleagues. *I can't be late for them.*

"Where's my purse?"

She looked on the kitchen counter, on the bar stool, on the couch, and on the floor next to the door to the garage where she typically dropped her purse after work. She found her black purse there, but not her new navy-blue one. She checked the dining room, the bathroom, and her car. *I can't find my purse!*

After ten minutes of searching, she gave up, grabbed her coffee and protein bar, and headed for her car. She placed the cup in one drink holder and the bar in the other. Then she realized she couldn't start the car. *I don't have the keys!*

Gabriella ran back into the house and grabbed her black purse. She dumped the contents on a little table: chewing gum, makeup, lipstick, a compact, mints, old receipts, outdated coupons and gift cards, lint, her daughter's soccer schedule, pencils, pens, a nail file, and an unwrapped cough drop—but *no keys!*

"Urgh!"

She started to panic but then remembered that her husband had lovingly made her a back-up set. He'd made a hook for them in the closet by the front door. *My back-up keys!* She ran to the closet only to discover an empty hook. She looked on the closet floor. *No keys!*

I guess I'll have to wake Mark and ask him if he's seen my keys. She started up the stairs. Halfway up, on the landing, she discovered her navy-blue purse.

"Thank God I found you!" She grabbed it and started down the stairs. When she reached into her bag, she felt the metal, but it felt different and heavy. She pulled it out—both sets of keys were tangled together! Her primary set and her back-up set were both in her purse. She knew what her engineer husband would say: "System failure."

Gabriela checked her phone for the time: 6:41. *Yikes! I'm going to be so late!*

Getting going in the morning can be a monumental task for someone with attention deficit disorder (ADD). In addition to losing keys, she might forget her computer with projects she needs for work. A person with ADD might leave his lunch on the kitchen counter or discover at the last minute that he doesn't have a pair of pants to wear that aren't wrinkled. Each small task of getting ready for work or school can be a source of frustration, distraction, and irritation.

Gabriela eventually made it to her university—fourteen minutes late for her meeting. She pulled the file for the meeting from her backpack and tossed it into her office. The backpack landed on her office chair—it was the only space free of papers, files, or books. There was one small side chair for her meetings with students, but it was crammed with tests that needed to be graded last week. Her desk was haphazardly organized into eleven stacks of papers. The bookshelves in her eight-foot-square office were jammed beyond capacity, with the inch or two below each shelf stuffed with more books wedged in horizontally. The gray-and-blue institutional carpet was littered with piles of research papers, notebooks, textbooks, boxes, and exams in various stacks—some were two feet high. A fourteen-inch path was cleared to provide access from the door to her chair. Her whiteboard had some brainstorming notes from three terms prior; now they were irrelevant. Beside the board was a two-year-old calendar featuring gorgeous photos of national parks. She had posted her office hours on her door, but they were out of date.

Josh slammed down another energy drink and punched off his video game console. The clock on the HD DVR announced that it was 1:31 a.m. He grabbed an accent pillow from the couch where he was seated and flung it across his living room like a flying disc. *I did it again! I didn't finish the work on the project that's due tomorrow!*

Instead of working on it, he lost three hours playing what was only supposed to be a "few minutes" of his favorite game. Josh thought video games helped him relax, but they were also a huge distraction. He would hyperfocus on the game, do well, and lose track of time. *If only I could do as well at work as I do on gaming,* he mused. He looked around the living room. For the first time in three hours—or maybe it was three days—he noticed the mess; it looked like a tornado had thrown his stuff all over—clothes, pizza boxes, junk mail, empty energy drink cans, and other debris. Some of it he didn't recognize as his. *Maybe the tornado blew in some of my neighbor's junk?* He tried to convince himself. *I can't be this messy!*

He took another look at the clock by his large flat-screen TV. The old feelings crept back in like a stinky, toxic fog. He felt like a failure. He felt disorganized and embarrassed about not completing tasks. He was afraid that people at work would talk about him being distracted, forgetful, late, and undependable. It made him feel like a loser. *These are the dark, familiar curses from college and high school.* He remembered his mom yelling at him when he was young: "Josh, why can't you put things away? I keep telling you to put your toys away in your toy box and don't leave them tossed all over the house! Why can't you remember to do that?"

He couldn't remember; he kept forgetting. Someone was always mad at him for being forgetful, messy, or disorganized or for saying things that were "inappropriate."

He was angry about the compilation of harsh criticism over the years, but he didn't want to give into it. He crushed the aluminum can in his fist. He grabbed a large trash bag from the kitchen and began tossing in the junk that had accumulated around him. He

was too frustrated to sleep, so he decided to spend an hour working on the project that was due on his boss's desk in a little more
than six hours.

Josh recalled his boss's comment from his last review: "Improve-
ment needed: giving attention to detail and follow-through."
He wanted to show her that he was working on these issues. He
opened up his laptop and the project folder on his desktop.
He stared at the document. It was just black words in Cambria
font on a white background. Words. Just words. It wasn't making
sense. *I need a snack to recharge my brain.*

Josh got up from the couch and went to the kitchen. He found
some cheese and crackers and took them back to the couch. After
he took a few bites, the words on the screen started to focus. They
started to make sense. It was now 2:14 a.m., and he was just getting started. *I have to finish this project, even if I have to stay up all
night. That's why they invented coffee.*

By 4:35 a.m., he was blurry-eyed but not beaten. The concepts
and words came to him, and he was able to finish his report,
including the statistical graphs and visuals that his boss had
requested. He saved it, sent it to his printer, and headed for bed.
*I have just enough time to sleep for an hour before I have to get up
and shower.*

At 5:45 a.m., his electric shaver purred, trimming the stubborn
stubble on his chin. *I look exhausted.* Josh stared at his reflection in
the mirror—faint half-moons underscored his bloodshot eyes, and
two new wrinkles seemed to have appeared on his forehead over-
night. *I have to break this last-minute panic, or it's going to cost me
my job.* Staring closer in the mirror, he thought, *I think it's causing*

me to age faster. He clicked the shaver off and muttered, "I need to get help."

Josh has ADD. On his lunch break that day, he called a therapist about an appointment. On the phone, he told him, "I'm tired of my procrastination, my lack of follow-through, and the subtle but ever-present feeling that I'm a failure. I don't want to feel like a loser. I want to feel confident and focused and meet my goals."

He felt comfortable talking with the therapist and made the wise decision to schedule an appointment. After all, ADD is a neurological disorder that makes it challenging for those with the condition to sustain focus and effort, take initiative with tasks, and organize their work and personal lives. The most common symptoms are impulsivity, distractibility, and hyperactivity. ADD is not caused by laziness, weak character, or lack of self-discipline. It's not correlated with intelligence; in fact, many people with ADD have high IQs. ADD is a democratic condition affecting all ethnicities and genders, regardless of circumstance.

The following is a conversation between Josh and his therapist that gives us insight into the struggles a person with ADD faces.

"My brother and I almost got into a fight while we were on vacation in the mountains of Colorado. My parents had rented a large cabin for us to be together, bond, and make happy memories with the grandkids," Josh told his therapist later that week. "But I think we almost destroyed it."

"What happened?"

"Eric is my older brother, and he picked on me as a kid. My mom always sided with me, and my dad sided with Eric. It made home life tense. Eric knows how to push my buttons. He sailed through high school, college, and graduate school and landed a sweet job, while I spent five years languishing in community college before I quit. He would call me 'stupid,' 'loser,' and 'lazy.' He used himself as the measure, and I didn't measure up. So I just avoided him, but now that he's married and has kids, I want to be part of their lives, so I agreed to go on this family vacation. My mom begged me to bury the hatchet and go. I almost buried the hatchet—right into my brother's skull!"

"Wow! That's intense. Go on."

"Eric wanted to control the schedule, even though our parents were paying for the vacation. For some reason, he thinks his ideas are the best and everyone should just follow him. He wanted us to go on this lame hike, and I just wanted to relax on the deck of the cabin and enjoy the view. He was going on and on about the beauty of this hike, wild animals we might see, and a waterfall that has a pool you can swim in. He was jabbering on and on about it until I couldn't handle it and said, 'Get to the point already!'

"Everyone in the cabin stopped what they were doing and watched the drama unfold. Eric stopped midsentence and challenged me: 'You want to make me?'

"His wife and kids looked up from their table game and stared. Eric puffed out his chest, stood up straight, and stepped toward me. He looked like he wanted to fight me in front of the entire family. I just wanted him to shut up. He thinks the best idea is *his* idea, and I can't stand it when he doesn't stop talking. It makes me see red."

"Does it feel like he's forcing his will on you?"

"Yeah, it reminds me of how he picked on me as a kid. He's just a bully, but now it's decades later, and he's still a jerk! So I stood up and said, 'Bring it!'"

Josh looked down at the carpet and sighed. "My mom started to cry, and my dad stood up," he continued, "but he didn't say anything. I wish I would have turned and walked out, but I swore at Eric, called him a name, and didn't back down. I just blurted out some stuff I really don't remember, but I do remember my mom crying and Eric's wife and kids looking frightened. Instead of being fun Uncle Josh, I reacted and became scary Uncle Josh."

"So much for building your relationship with your nephew and niece. What would you like to have done instead of reacting and scaring the kids?" asked his therapist.

"I'm not sure. That's why I'm here. I need to do things differently."

The therapist pulled out a whiteboard the size of a laptop. He wrote *scapegoat* on it. "Do you know what a scapegoat is?" he asked.

"Yeah, it's the goat that gets sacrificed. It's the person who gets blamed for all the problems in the family. I'm the scapegoat in my family. I'm seen as the cause of our drama and chaos."

"Sometimes that happens in a family. You become what therapists call the 'designated patient.' The family learns to revolve around one person. Your mom might try to rescue you, but your dad thinks she's doing too much, and your brother thinks you should change. And you are likely to be triggered by Eric's rants because you don't have time for them."

"Exactly! Have you peeked in our windows? That's exactly what goes on in our wacky family."

The therapist wrote *impatient* on the whiteboard. "It sounds like you don't have the patience for Eric's long speeches. Your impatience causes you to react. You probably feel bullied when he's taking up all the airtime yakking about whatever he wants to. These two things are typical of someone with ADD—receiving blame and impatience. The third characteristic of someone with ADD is impulsiveness." He wrote *impulsive* on the board. "When you get triggered, it's difficult for you to control your speech and behavior. This lack of impulse control can add to drama and blame because your level of reaction might be more observable than Eric's. In fact, Eric might be more hostile and mean-spirited, but you *look* like you are out of control, and therefore you become *the problem*."

Josh nodded his head in agreement. "Exactly! Eric might appear to be cool, but his attacks are persistent and covert. He's like a ninja assassin attempting to kill my self-worth."

The therapist nodded. "And a person with ADD has a fourth characteristic." He wrote *low EI* on the board. "Some people with ADD are easily distracted and don't pick up emotional and facial cues that other people might be sending. As a result, they have low EI, or emotional intelligence. This has nothing to do with your IQ—it's the ability to communicate to others how you feel and to understand others' feelings. Empathy is one factor of emotional intelligence. Sometimes people with ADD react in a way that might seem impulsive to others because they didn't *read the room*. They say something without realizing that it could have a negative impact on another person."

"Like me blurting out those things to Eric in Colorado. I didn't even think about what I was saying and how it would hurt my mom and Eric's wife and kids. I just wanted to stand up to Eric. I can see what you are saying. My ex-girlfriend told me, 'You need to notice the atmosphere of the room and the mood of the people in it before shooting off your mouth.' She was right, and that's why she's my ex. She couldn't handle my reactions and hurtful words." He looked intently at the whiteboard. "Yup, that's me—scapegoat, impatient, weak impulse control, and not always the most sensitive guy. Am I doomed to be a mess, or can I change?"

Gabriela and Josh are real people with ADD. Their names have been changed to protect their privacy. They both need to learn how to live with ADD, and they both need someone to love and understand them. But they aren't destined to lead troubled lives. They aren't "doomed" just because they have these traits. ADD is a condition, not a curse. It's a syndrome, not a sentence.

For years, ADD was viewed only as a disorder of hyperactive boys. Now we know that there are various kinds of ADD, and an estimated *eighteen million people* in the United States have been diagnosed with ADD—children, teens, and adults, male and female.

Ten Myths about ADD

1. ADD is something you'll grow out of.
2. ADD is overdiagnosed. It's just kids being kids and adults being distracted.
3. ADD is a trendy, pop-culture disease du jour. It's just an excuse for a lack of self-control.

4. The overdiagnosis of ADD reflects our slap-on-a-label and pop-a-pill culture. We want a quick fix. We are too busy to work on a more complex solution.

5. The whole ADD epidemic is overplayed. It's a minor issue getting major airtime.

6. ADD was invented and sustained in America. It's really not an issue elsewhere.

7. ADD is an excuse for a lack of a strong work ethic. It is residue from a generation of entitlement.

8. ADD is really an indication of a lack of character.

9. ADD is a result of ineffective parents and anxious teachers who are focused on the wrong things. Instead of focusing on feelings and psychology, they should be focused on discipline and traditional values.

10. The best treatment for ADD is medication alone.

Ten Facts about ADD

1. Many people with ADD are never hyperactive.

2. Less than half of those with ADD undergo some form of treatment.[1]

3. Higher intelligence typically delays the diagnosis of ADD. Bright students with ADD can partially tune into their teachers and still perform well enough—until they get to a grade or subject that requires their full focus and sustained concentration.

4. ADD is the most common educational and behavioral challenge among school-age children. According to the Centers for Disease Control and Prevention, 13.2 percent of boys and 5.6 percent of girls have been diagnosed.[2] The *New York*

Times recently reported that 20 percent of teenage boys are diagnosed with ADD, and half of them are medicated.[3]

5. Many children, teens, and adults don't know they have ADD and have never had a professional diagnosis.[4]

6. ADD is more prevalent among foster and adopted children than among the general population.[5]

7. ADD affects all ethnic groups, socioeconomic strata, degrees of intelligence, educational levels, and geographies.[6]

8. About one-third of the ADD population outgrows the disorder, leaving two-thirds who have it throughout adulthood.[7]

9. Untreated ADD can be troublesome: 52 percent of untreated adults and teens abuse drugs and alcohol, while 33 percent never finish high school (in contrast to the national average of 8.7 percent). People with the disorder are twice as likely to smoke cigarettes and more than four times as likely to be arrested. Three out of four have interpersonal problems due to their untreated ADD. They get more speeding tickets and have more motor vehicle accidents and instances of driving without a valid license. They are more likely to be injured—up to five times more than those without ADD.[8] Parents of ADD children divorce three times more than the general population, and people with ADD are more likely to divorce.[9]

10. ADD can be an asset, especially when it is identified early and treated. People with ADD typically have high energy, spunk, creativity, resilience, persistence, and the ability to hyperfocus. They are passionate and work well under

pressure. They multitask, frequently engage in nonlinear thinking, and are our champion athletes, actors, and CEOs.

ADD is not a problem that needs to be solved but a condition that needs to be understood, appreciated, and leveraged.

One of my family's favorite movies is the animated Pixar beauty *Up*. Do you remember the scene when Carl and Russell discover Dug, the talking dog? Dug has a distinctive characteristic besides the ability to talk. He's passionate, engaging, and intelligent and has leadership skills. But right in the middle of fervently talking about something he's fully engaged in, Dug will turn and shout, "Squirrel!" Getting distracted is common in people (and dogs?) with ADD. Since the movie came out in 2009, my family has adopted saying "Squirrel!" as a humorous way to point out that someone has gotten sidetracked. Like Dug in *Up*, those of us with ADD can have many "squirrels" that catch our attention and divert us from our intended task or conversation.

Gene is an intelligent, creative man who came to see me because he could easily identify with Dug. He had lots of distracting squirrels popping up in his life. What follows is a conversation I had with him.

"I'm here because my wife asked me to get help," admitted Gene, a successful fortysomething creative director for an advertising agency. "I do well at work. I'm responsible for leading our team to generate new ideas to pitch our clients. Creative, artsy types surround me, and it's easy for most of us to get sidetracked. I might have ADD, although I've never been professionally diagnosed. But our son, Grayson, was having trouble paying attention at school, so we had him diagnosed, and the psychologist said he had ADD. He listed the symptoms, and it sounded just like me: easily distracted, forgetful, impulsive, innovative, and high energy."

"How can I help?" I asked.

Gene looked down at his designer Italian loafers. "I'm embarrassed to admit it ... uh ... my wife asked me ... she asked me because of what happened last week." He cleared his throat. "I lost my kid. It was like a scene from a movie. On my way home from work, I was supposed to pick up Grayson from soccer practice. My wife texted me at 5 p.m. to remind me, but on the way home, I decided to swing into my favorite coffee place and get an iced coffee. I got it to go, but as I drove home, I was drawn into a hilarious comedy routine on satellite radio. It was a long bit, but it made the drive home go fast—so fast that I drove right past the soccer field. I didn't realize I had forgotten until I got home and my wife asked, 'Where's Grayson?' I sped back to the field, twenty-five minutes late. Grayson was there with his friend Hunter and Hunter's mom. She didn't look too thrilled. I apologized to her, to Grayson, and when I got home, to my wife, but she said I need to do something about this because it happens too much."

"What's that?"

"I get sidetracked. I'm easily distracted. I find it difficult to complete a task unless I'm really into it. I can hyperfocus at work because I'm passionate about it, I'm good at it, and it's fun. But anything else is likely to be detoured. My whole life is one long sidetrack!"

Gene's story will be familiar to adults with ADD. His default setting was "squirrel," or "easily distracted." He might have had the best intentions and a high degree of commitment to stay on task, but something would come along and throw him off course. His wife was fed up with it; she wanted him to change. But when Gene tried to focus on focusing, it typically backfired. For some reason, when he put a lot of effort into being laser-focused, his mind would shut down, freeze, or offer some delectable diversion instead. Gene felt like there was a civil war going on in his brain.

"Gene, you aren't broken," I told him. "You aren't defective. It sounds like you do, in fact, have ADD, but you can leverage it. You can *harness the power.* I like to say, 'ADD is a difference, not a disorder.' ADD is a condition, not a curse. It's a syndrome, not a sentence."

"So there's hope for me?" asked Gene.

"Yes, Gene, there is hope."

CHAPTER TWO

The ADD Club

"I was twenty-seven years old when my doctor told me I had ADD. I didn't like the label. I didn't want a *diagnosis.* I didn't want to be different or have a *disorder* or have some excuse, but I did want help," Hayden told me on his first appointment at my office. "My impulsiveness had ruined my relationship with my girlfriend; she's now my ex. My lack of follow-through kept me from getting promoted at work. My lack of focus and disorganization could be seen in my townhouse, my car, and my finances. My life was messy, but I didn't think I had a medical problem. But then it hit me—*I have ADD.* I didn't like the stigma. I didn't want to be part of this group. I didn't choose to be in this club, but here I am."

For the last twenty-five years, physicians, psychiatrists, psychologists, and therapists have typically delivered the diagnosis of ADD to their patients as "a problem," alerting patients to the strong possibility of a lifelong struggle with challenging symptoms and prescribing a stimulant as the conventional treatment for the "pathology." The fact that we call it a diagnosis presupposes an illness and therefore a need for a prescription. I like what Dr. Dale Archer writes in his book *The ADHD Advantage: What You Thought Was a Diagnosis May Be Your Greatest Strength:*

Of course, the awareness that you have ADHD can actually be a good thing. But the problem is that we are calling it a diagnosis, which automatically suggests the need for treatment, which is almost always in the form of meds. A diagnosis also suggests a kind of uniformity to the trait that simply does not exist. We're overlooking too many variables in the range of symptoms and severity. It's *not* one-size-fits-all. While there is no question ADHD is a prevalent trait, it is not black-and-white. There are multiple shades of gray, and yet our culture keeps putting everyone in the same box when the effects of the trait are complex and nuanced and rarely require what has become the standard treatment—a pill.[1]

Hayden shifted in his chair and reached for the disposable cup of water next to him. He wore stylish designer glasses, skinny jeans, and a casual collared shirt. He began stroking his beard.

"So you don't like the label or being forced to be part of the ADD club?" I inquired.

"Nope. I could live without it. I'm not really a joiner, so I definitely don't want to be part of a club identified by its problem—by its pathology. I'm kind of a rogue, so I don't like being forced to be in a group or on a team. When I was in high school, I only did individual sports. So you can see why I don't want to be identified with a group with a 'disorder.'"

"Definitely. I understand. Nobody likes labels. For many people, when they hear 'ADD,' they think it's a liability. It has a negative reputation, frequently characterized as unreliable, impulsive, unorganized, and unfocused—but what if we looked at the other side of ADD? Just like a coin, there are two sides. The complementary side is that many people with ADD are highly energetic, resilient, visionary entrepreneurs who think outside the box. They are positive and very passionate. They can be successful in a variety of roles. And frankly, Hayden, a lot of them are rogues too. Your club has some of the world's best pioneers, explorers, inventors, artists, CEOs, and leaders. They take risks and go where no man has gone before."

He smiled at the reference. "Yeah, I like to take risks. I hate to be bored. Can someone really learn to make ADD work *for* him rather than *against* him? I thought once you were diagnosed, you were stuck. You were doomed. It's like a chronic illness."

"Yes, you can learn new habits that will maximize your strengths and minimize your weaknesses. You can tap into skills you have that others might not, like creativity, responding well under pressure, and the ability to hyperfocus. Can you get lost in a project if you are interested in it?"

"Absolutely!" He smiled. "I was designing a new look for a website for one of my favorite clients. I had discovered the perfect color scheme, scale, font, colors, and layout. I got so lost in it that I worked until eight p.m.—totally in the zone. Not a moment of distraction or boredom."

"That's what I'm talking about. In that case, ADD is an asset. It doesn't have to be a disease. It's just a difference. Not every difference is a dysfunction. Your brain functions differently. You have a low threshold for boredom. If something isn't capturing your interest, your brain tells you to find something more provocative."

"Exactly. My mind seems to run at higher RPMs. It's like a Porsche that likes to go fast and furious and take the curves hard. I like the challenge. I like the speed. But if it's slow, I'll get distracted and go off the road. I can't tell you how many rabbit trails I've taken at work because I was bored."

"I don't like the label *ADD* either. It's negative. I mean, it has 'deficit' as its middle name and 'disorder' as it's last name. I can see why you don't want to be part of that club. But what if we gave it a different name? We can be rogues ourselves and rename it. How about if we call it what it really is for you? You have ALBT."

"Alternative living … what?"

"Nice guess. But it's a name I created because I think it's more descriptive for some people—*ALBT*—active low boredom threshold. Your high energy, enthusiasm, and curiosity keep your mind active, spinning at high RPMs like a Porsche. But your threshold for boredom is low. If something doesn't engage you, you will search for something that does. Hayden, you are in the ALBT club!"

"Well, that already sounds better."

"That's because it has better marketing than ADD, which has been given an undeserved negative reputation."

"So how do I start turning this difference into my greatest strength?" Hayden asked with a smile.

"There is unlimited potential for people with ADD," I answered. "The key to a meaningful life is acceptance—*because of*, not *despite*, ADD. You are unique. Be content with your custom design. There is no one else like you! You are a one-of-a-kind combination of personality, genetics, brain chemistry, and passions. Your brain might not work like a 'typical' brain, but it doesn't matter. What matters is discovering the hope you have by leveraging your brain's characteristics as strengths, knowing your limits, discovering the best way for you to learn, and plotting your education and career path to fit your unique design. You don't have to fit into the box that parents, teachers, peers, and others say is *normal.* You can be a rogue. ADD is not a sentence; it's a different way of thinking. Embrace the difference."

Vive la Différence

What is the difference between a person with ADD and someone without it?

Someone with ADD has a brain that reacts differently to stimulation. ADD is a combination of brain chemistry and genetics that affects dopamine levels and the brain's neuropathways. The stress of a fender bender, the pressure of a deadline, or the adrenaline of a risky action sport might create panic, trepidation, or anxiety in someone without ADD; for a person with ADD, these situations are likely to generate laser-focus, energy, a rush, or euphoria.

We have friends who are firefighters, police officers, paramedics, emergency room physicians, trauma nurses, salespeople, and delivery truck drivers. All of them are successful and love their careers. They seldom find work boring because they are putting out fires (literally and figuratively). They spring into duty with focus, energy, enthusiasm, and efficiency. They are top performers in their respective fields, and they all have ADD.

ADD traits don't have to be changed or suppressed. ADD is a natural part of our human condition and sometimes helps people excel at work. ADD is not a problem to be fixed but a unique way of thinking that needs to be understood, loved, and leveraged for its strengths.

For many of us, working a shift in the ER would make us want to check in as a patient; we couldn't handle the pressure. But for people with ADD, the thrill of life-or-death situations creates a chemical reaction within their brains that helps them focus and jump into action without hesitation. This adrenalin-fired work environment isn't for everyone. Some of us prefer a serene cubicle with drawer organizers, paper clips stored by size, extra staples in the back, and color-coded files—no clutter, no surprises, and no drama. Not all of us need a lot of excitement at work. We don't all embrace risk and spontaneity. Not all of us can generate creative ideas, concepts, and designs. It takes both kinds of people to make things happen in our society. Men and women with ADD play a vital role as creatives, innovators, risk-takers, leaders, explorers, and entrepreneurs. We need these folks to push the boundaries, to imagine, to rattle the status quo, and to ask "What if?"

Travis's Journey

Sometimes parents feel that they have failed because their child has ADD. That was Wendy's experience. She had expended so much energy and effort on her son, Travis, but it didn't seem to matter. What follows is our extended conversation.

"I went online and saw that my son Travis is getting mostly Ds and is missing assignments," said Wendy. "I'm calling you because I heard you work with teens with ADD. Our family physician diagnosed Travis with ADD, but that was years ago, and we haven't put him on meds or done anything with it since he was in sixth grade. By the way, we gave him an extra year before starting him in kindergarten, and he flunked fourth grade, so he's two years older than some of his classmates. When can you see him? The sooner, the better?"

This is a typical call for me. Parents and teachers might notice that a child is displaying symptoms of ADD at a young age but assume it's minor. Teachers might rationalize the behavior by saying things like "He'll grow out of it" or "He needs more discipline or structure." Some parents do nothing until their child's behavior or grades become so abysmal, they have to address the issue. That was the case with Travis. Standing six foot three and weighing three hundred pounds as a sophomore got him a position on the varsity football team in the fall of his junior year. He was a second-string guard. He liked the camaraderie and prestige of being on the varsity football team at his high school, but he didn't like the practices. Travis had below a C average when the progress report came out midway through the season and couldn't play in the games. If he didn't raise his grades, his coach would cut him from the team. Wendy called me in desperation.

"We want you to fix his ADD. We want you to help organize his brain and his schedule, help him with his messy notebook, and teach him how to use his assignment app," she pleaded.

A few days later, I met Travis. He was bigger than I expected, even though he walked with slumped shoulders and shuffled his feet. He plopped down on the couch in my office and extended his size fourteens in my direction.

"Do you have a difficult time finding kicks?"

He smiled. "Yes, I had to get these at the outlets. I can't find fourteens at the mall, but the outlets always have my size and bigger, and they're cheaper."

"So I heard you can't play football until you bring your grades up."

"Yup ..." he flipped his phone over in his massive hand. "It's all good. I'm going to quit anyway. I hate the practices, and the only reason I endured them was to dress and maybe play in the games. I'm not like most of the other guys. I'm just big. I'm really not that fast or coordinated. Some of them have been playing since they were eight. I just started as a freshman. Plus, I'm really not into it."

"Why do you say that?" I asked.

"Well, a lot of my teammates eat, breathe, and talk football. It's their life. They are obsessed with it. When they aren't doing that, they are playing the *Madden NFL* video game. Some dream of playing in college and the NFL. I don't," admitted Travis.

"What do you dream about? What is your passion?"

"Do you really want to know?"

"Yeah, I do."

"Well, it's not being in school, I can tell you that. I hate school. I know I'm not supposed to be a hater, but how else do I say it? 'I have a very strong dislike for school'? I want to get my GED and be done. School is such a pain."

"What do your parents want for you?"

"They want me to bring my grades up, become a good student, and keep playing football because it *teaches me character.* They want me to graduate and go to community college. They are really pushing the college deal, but I can't even get through high school, and I'm in easy classes."

"Why college? What would you study?"

"I have no idea. I'd be the first in the family to go to college. My parents didn't go, their parents didn't go, but for some freakin' reason, *I'm* supposed to go to college and break the chain of dumbness." He smiled.

"That's funny. But it's also a lot of pressure. Let's say you quit football and you suddenly have twenty hours a week that you don't have now. You could spend ten of those raising your grades, so what would you do with the other ten?"

"Our neighborhood has really deep backyards. The houses are crappy, but the yards are huge. So there's a neighbor two doors down named Charlie. He's an old guy—older than my dad—and he's got a full-blown machine shop in his yard. I like to go down there and tinker around. I've been going there since I was a kid. Charlie taught me to solder, weld, use the drill press, machine parts, use the lathe, and work on cars. He has all the tools. I'm helping him on a project car now. He rebuilds it, sells it, and buys another. It's fun. I'd rather be there than school or football."

"Would you spend your free ten hours there at Charlie's?"

"Yeah, that would be fun."

"Okay, so here's the deal. You need the reward of going to Charlie's, but you also need to spend the same amount of time bringing your grades up. It's one for one. One hour of homework equals one hour at Charlie's. If you can do some homework at school during your free time and lunch, record the time you spent on it. If you can do that for four days a week, you can binge at Charlie's starting Friday night and all day Saturday and Sunday. But you have to do the work first and then reward yourself with time at Charlie's.

Keep a record in your phone so you don't cheat. And go online and see what's missing and ask each teacher what you can do to bring your grades up. Sometimes it's easier than you think. Can you do those three things?"

"Yeah, for sure!" Travis said enthusiastically.

"Okay, write them down in your phone and put reminders beside them with alarms."

Travis's thumbs went flying, adding his assignment to his phone. "Okay, done."

"Great. See you next week."

Travis talked his parents into letting him quit football to focus on his grades. It worked. Within two weeks, he had a C average and was hanging out at Charlie's having fun rebuilding an old Ford truck.

His mom called me and said, "We are happy with his grades. Thanks for your work with him, but we really want Travis to go to college. If he just works up to his potential, he can do it."

"What would he study?"

"I don't know, but it would help him get a better job."

"Like what?"

"I don't know."

"Have you noticed that Travis is stubborn, and you can't make him do anything that he doesn't want to do?"

Wendy laughed. "Oh, yeah! That's the story of my life. I gave up when he was two."

"But if he really is into something, you can't pull him away from it, right?"

"Exactly. Hey, you really know Travis."

"Not that well, but I know ADD when I see it. Travis can hyper-focus on something he is passionate about, but you can't coerce him into doing something he doesn't want to do."

"Like homework."

"And football and college."

"Yeah … you're right. So what are we supposed to do?"

"I have an idea. Travis is a tactile-kinesthetic-visual learner. He learns by touching, moving, and designing things. That's why he loves going to Charlie's and why he really doesn't like conventional academics."

"Yeah, he's been a tinkerer since he was four. He'd rather do that than play with traditional toys—except for Legos. What's your idea?"

"Check out the ROP classes they offer down by the old airport. You can look them up online, and if you and Travis like what you see, schedule a visit and see if he likes the classes and the workshop there. It's designed for teens just like Travis, and it's affordable."

"Okay. What's ROP?"

"*ROP* stands for regional occupational program—it's run by the county. I'll send you the link. I've sent other teens there to take classes that you can't get at high school. They are very hands-on and build skills that will get Travis a job, and he won't need college."

"Are you sure?"

"Yes, just show it to him and take a tour."

A week later, I met with Travis.

"My mom and I went to the ROP place on Friday," he said.

"What did you think of it?" I asked.

"It was cool. They have some high-tech equipment and tools—stuff I want to learn how to use. Plus they have a certification in fabricating that looks good. I can get it in eighteen months if I start now and take a summer school class there. They have you do an internship in a machine shop or fabrication shop or some real business like that. So it's not like I'm sitting on my butt in some boring class."

"This sounds like it's your passion. Even though you have ADD, if you find something you are passionate about, you can hyperfocus, get in the zone, and do really well because you are in the flow."

"Yeah, I know what you're talking about. When Charlie and I were working on the truck on Saturday, I was there for twelve hours, and I never got bored. And I went back on Sunday for eight hours. It's fun. I like doing stuff with my hands. I like creating things in my head and then trying to make them. Oh, they also offer drafting at ROP, so I'll be able to take the stuff in my head, put my ideas into AutoCAD and make a drawing or a 3-D printout of the design, and then use the other digital machines to build it. How cool is that?"

We had discovered how to turn Travis's ADD into a strength. What some had called his "disorder" became the most powerful tool in his toolbox.

Eighteen months later, he graduated from high school and the ROP program with a certification in metal fabrication. A week later, he got an offer from an off-road fabricator shop specializing in making trucks and buggies for the Baja races. His starting salary was $75,000 a year, plus benefits—including working the Baja races! It was a gearhead's dream come true.

A few years later, Wendy called me to refer a friend, and she updated me on Travis: "He loves his job, and his boss loves him.

He's doing well, and he's got two promotions and is making six figures now! We had no idea you could make that kind of money, be happy, and have a career without going to college. Thanks for helping direct Travis down the education and career path that fits him."

Meet the Club

For many years, therapists saw ADD as strictly a childhood issue. But Dr. Alan Zametkin at the National Institute of Mental Health conducted his landmark study with adults, not children. This major study established a biological basis for ADD. Dr. Zametkin proved that the difference between a person with ADD and a person without is at the cellular level—a difference among the parts of the brain that regulate attention, emotion, and impulse control.[2]

Due to developments in neuroscience, we are now able to scan the brain and see how it works in real time. With brain imaging, we can observe how a brain with ADD consumes energy differently from a brain without ADD. For instance, the brain scan of a person with ADD might indicate lots of energy being consumed in one area of the brain but less energy consumed in the area assigned to focus and attention. It's not simply an issue of intelligence, laziness, motivation, or character, as some have erroneously judged; it's brain chemistry. The ADD club comprises various types of ADD, and each person has it on a continuum that ranges from very mild to very severe. This is important to remember if you are trying to understand someone with ADD: one size doesn't fit all. Each person's ADD experience is unique.

As a result, the ADD club is very diverse (more on that later). We are learning much about ADD, but there's still a lot we don't know. In fact, the exact biochemical mechanism underlying ADD remains unknown. Here are the facts we have now: Although environmental factors do influence the course of ADD over a lifetime, most practitioners in the field now agree that the characteristic problems of people with ADD stem from neurobiological malfunctioning. Our understanding of the biological components of the syndrome has revolutionized our thinking about ADD in the past fifteen years and shaped our ability to treat it effectively.[3]

Eighteen million people in the United States have ADD. There is typically one in every classroom, likely one at work, and one or more in each family. You might have ADD. If you do, you know the pain that goes with the label. You know the challenges you faced at school, in relationships, and now at work. In this book, we will identify the challenges adults with ADD face and teach you strategies to deal with them. If you love someone with ADD, we will show you how to understand them and the skills you can use to enhance your relationship.

Think about the common positive traits of the ADD club. Instead of focusing on the disadvantages of ADD, I like to flip them around and see them as strengths. People with ADD can do the following:

- remain calm under intense pressure and in chaos
- multitask
- hyperfocus on something that fascinates him or her
- engage in creative, nonlinear thinking
- take calculated risks

They have several positive personality traits as well:

- entrepreneurial
- adventurous
- energetic
- resilient
- positive and hopeful
- spontaneous
- often artistic and visually oriented

These abilities and characteristics are vital to our society. Without the ADD club, we'd have a huge dip in our levels of excitement and innovation.

CHAPTER THREE

You Aren't Alone

A few years ago, I was speaking to a large group of young moms in Malibu, California.

"If you want a healthy family, you need to be aligned with the same purpose," I told them. "If you are a single mom, you need to be aligned with yourself. You need to be consistent. If you are married, you need to align with your spouse around the purpose of your family. You want to be on the same page. You want to have the same goal. As a family coach, I've come to see that there are three kinds of families. Each has a different focus. The first kind is the child-centered family, in which the child becomes the prince or princess and the parents become servants. These parents run all over the globe trying to make their child comfortable, happy, and protected from all negative influences, especially boredom. The child is put on a pedestal. He or she is exalted. He or she becomes an idol."

I noticed a few moms nudging each other and whispering. I continued, "The problem with this kind of family is that the kid knows, at some level, that he or she shouldn't be on the pedestal and will act out to demonstrate this. And he or she is likely to be insecure because at any moment, he or she could fall from the pedestal; this is a frightening notion because he or she has never really experienced discomfort."

The women were actively taking notes. A few were looking at each other. I noticed quite a few shifted uncomfortably in their seats.

"The second kind of family is parent-centered, where the parent or parents' life becomes the focus, and the child is viewed as an accessory. The parent might be wrapped up in his or her career or pastime and have very little bandwidth to connect with his or her child in a meaningful way. The child might have time with his parent, but it's spent doing what the parent wants to do. 'Come watch me play ball,' or 'You get to stay at this hotel with a pool while I'm there for a conference,' or 'We're going to the desert this weekend, and you get to watch while Daddy rides his motorcycle.' The child in these families is viewed as a symbol—an object, an extension of the parent, a Mini-Me of the parent—reinforcing the parent's *brand*. A child raised in a parent-centered family is likely to grow up angry and resentful.

"These are the most common kinds of families in our country. But common doesn't mean healthy. The third kind of family is the healthiest because it has the right focus—not the child, not the parent, but something that is truly worth being the center of your home."

I paused for effect and smiled at the moms. All eyes were on me. "The third and healthiest kind of family is the Christ-centered family, where it's not about the kid or the parent but about everyone becoming more like Christ—speaking the truth, showing mercy, living out grace, demonstrating love, and offering forgiveness. I know that not all of you are faith-based people, so consider this if you prefer a secular alternative: the center of your family needs to be timeless principles that have proven useful in societies, relationships, and families. In either case, it's not child-centered or parent-centered; it's about child and parent desiring to learn and grow together. In other words, it's not about you."

I wrapped up my presentation and walked toward my book table. Before I got there, a woman ran up to me and exclaimed, "I have a child-centered family, and it's driving me crazy! It's out of control, and my husband and I don't know what to do. I understand you make house calls. When can you come? Can you come today? Can you come right after this?" She paused to catch her breath.

"Yes, I make house calls. Let me check my schedule. What's your name?" I extended my hand.

"Oh, I'm sorry. I didn't mean to barge in like this, but I'm desperate. My name is Topanga."

I smiled at the name.

"I know, the name. I grew up here in Malibu. My parents were artsy, hippie types, hence *Topanga*. So when can you come?"

I checked my calendar on my phone. "I can come Thursday night."

Topanga's experience illustrates some of the struggles parents with children with attention deficit disorder (ADD) encounter, especially in a child-centered family. Here's what happened.

A few days later, I knocked on her door. While I waited, I noticed the tranquility of the surrounding landscape. I heard the waves crash on the point, I heard seagulls squawk, and I drew in the fresh salty air. All was serene—until the door opened. Before I could step across the threshold, a three-foot marauder ran toward me, screaming at the top of his lungs.

"He's excited to see you!" Topanga yelled over the screaming.

"It looks like it. Maybe he—"

Pop! Pop! The mini martial artist punched me in the groin. Twice!

"Oh, I can tell he really likes you," said Topanga.

What does he do to people he doesn't like? I thought as I bent over and attempted to recover from the surprise attack.

"Damian!" she yelled. "Damian, come here and meet Mr. Tim!"

After a few minutes of her yelling and threatening, Damian settled down, stopped running, and came up to me. I introduced myself, extended my right hand, and protected myself with the other hand. It seemed strange to me that Topanga didn't bother to correct him for his aggressiveness. *She's right—this kid is out of control.*

She sent him upstairs to find his dad and then said, "He's almost got himself kicked out of pre-K. The director called me this week with the second warning. Three strikes and he's out. I don't know what to do. My parents were very permissive and let me and my siblings do anything. If I had any discipline, it was from one nanny, but neither my husband nor I know how to handle Damian."

Perhaps you should have picked a different name rather than naming him after a child of hell, I thought.

"I had trouble in school too. I would daydream or draw when I was supposed to be doing my work. In high school, if it was a nice day, my friends and I would ditch school and go to the beach. The school disciplined me for being truant, but my parents didn't. I don't think I learned how to be a parent. I'm just now figuring out how to be an adult. The same is true with my husband, Rob. We spent a decade having fun, traveling, and partying. I didn't have Damian until I was thirty-seven."

Note to self, I thought, *Mom probably has ADD too.*

Rob and Damian joined us, and I led them through a quick discussion of what a healthy family looks like—focusing on being consistent, having consequences, and not allowing Damian to be the center of the family. We did some role-playing, I wrote down some ideas on their whiteboard, and together we came up with some basic expectations and consequences. Damian participated and seemed to like the structure. After an hour, Rob took him upstairs for a bath.

"Thanks for coming. This has been so helpful." Topanga pointed to the notes she had been taking in her spiral notebook. "I've learned more in the last hour on how to parent than in all my seven years getting my master's."

"You're welcome," I said. "What is your master's in?"

"Marriage and family therapy. But I never did get my license—just the degree."

I almost fell out of my chair. She might have had it in her head, but she didn't have it in her home!

Topanga had undiagnosed ADD. After a few sessions with her in which she told me about her childhood, I strongly suspected her parents had it too. Damian was a third-generation person with ADD.

You might be able to relate to the confusion, tension, and energy of having ADD or having a child with ADD. You aren't alone.

The Swirl

A child or parent should not be the center of a family, particularly a child or a parent with ADD. When a family revolves around one person, like Topanga's, it creates what we call "the swirl"—an escalation of drama in which more energy is invested in and more resources are allocated to the *designated patient*, or the axis of the energy of the family. A family becomes unhealthy when it revolves around one person; it becomes frenetic when it revolves around a person with ADD.

If your focus is primarily on one family member, he or she could become an idol. Without knowing it, he or she becomes your favorite. He is special. She requires more of your time. Watch out for idolatry—even in the form of love. This can lead to entitlement, learned helplessness, insecurity, jealousy, and resentment among the nonspecial family members. See the following example from Genesis: "Now Israel loved Joseph more than any of his other sons, because he had been born to him in his old age; and he made an ornate robe for him. When his brothers saw that their father loved him more than any of them, they hated him and could not speak a kind word to him" (37:3–4).

Israel (a.k.a. Jacob) really loved the baby of the family, Joseph. He had a special coat made for him. He treated him with favor. Jacob's brothers resented all the attention he received. *It wasn't fair.* When they had the opportunity, they threw Joseph in a pit. At that point, they could have killed him to get rid of all the "Joseph is special" fuss. Instead, they sold him into slavery.

Siblings will do bizarre and unkind things in an attempt to level the playing field. If one child is receiving all the attention, siblings will seek to destroy, alienate, tease, or abuse the idol of the family.

Favoritism is a subtle, toxic poison that can contaminate a family. There is a difference between making accommodations for a child with ADD and allowing him or her to become the center of the family. As you would with a child with a physical disability, you provide resources for adaptive abilities, but your family identity and focus aren't on the one person with the disability. This concept might be difficult to understand if you are a caring parent with a child with ADD.

It's challenging to find a healthy boundary between supporting and enabling your child. Support means making accommodations, providing adaptations, and empowering your child to make decisions for herself. Enabling means doing things for him that he could do for himself. It's seeing your child with ADD as helpless and fragile and incapable of thinking for herself. It's assuming responsibility for your child's life. Enabling looks like caring, but it's controlling, and it robs a child of developing a sense of ownership and empowerment.

This was the situation with my client Donna. The following is our extended conversation.

"I know you think you are caring and protecting, but I think your son Joey has learned to work the system," I said to Donna, a first-time client.

"Are you saying I do too much for him?" asked the mother of four adult sons. "But I have to! He was picked on by his older brothers—all three of them. He was just a toddler, and they were mercilessly abusing him. And when he got into school and got in trouble for not sitting still, not paying attention, or showing off, his brothers teased him for his bad grades and made comments about his bad behavior. So what was I supposed to do? I had to protect him from his own brothers."

"Do they think it was fair?"

"Oh, no! They say I play favorites—that I love Joey more than them. He's the baby of the family, and I focused on him too much, according to them. Now, as adults, they hate each other. Joey feels worthless, and his brothers think he's a loser because they say he can't hold down a job, can't complete anything, and lives on my dime."

"What do you do to support him? How is he living on your dime?"

"Lou, my husband, and I gave him money to start his own business, and we bought a townhouse for him. He's supposed to pay us rent, but for the last year, he hasn't because his company isn't profitable yet."

"How old are he and the company?"

"He's thirty-eight, and the company is seven years old."

"So he didn't finish college, he lives in a home that you pay for, and you probably subsidize his life because his company doesn't turn a profit yet."

"Yes, we give him an allowance of two thousand dollars a month, but he's complaining that it's not enough."

"That sounds like enabling to me. Joey's learned to be helpless and dependent. Have you considered that overfocusing on him might have created a codependent situation—making him less capable and confident—and created more tension in your family because of his brothers' resentment?"

Donna looked down. She started to cry. She reached for a tissue and cleared her throat. "I'm offended by you calling me *codependent* … but you're not the first. Lou was a compulsive gambler, and I learned about codependency in Gamblers Anonymous. It's a support group for spouses with partners who are addicted to gambling. It was there I discovered that I *loved too much*—that I was enabling Lou's addiction. I had to make some difficult choices. But now Lou is sober—I mean, he still drinks, but he doesn't gamble. It almost ruined our marriage. The years of his deepest addiction were the years the boys were at home." She brushed a tissue across her cheek, wiping off the tears, and slowly raised her head.

"Is Lou impulsive?" I asked. "Does he like the adrenaline buzz he gets from gambling?"

"Oh, yeah. He normally moves slowly, but if there was a chance to go to Vegas, he'd drop his work midday and go without notice. I'd be home with four boys, and he'd call from the casino to let me know he wasn't going to be home."

"Do you think Joey gets that from him? He sounds like he might have similar issues."

"Well, he does. Not everyone in the family knows. We try to keep it a secret from his brothers and everyone else, but Joey was in treatment twice for addiction to opiates. He's sober now, thank God, but I think it's his way of self-medicating to hide the pain from being wounded by his brothers and his hurtful experiences at school."

"So there's a lot of drama in your family. For years, there was a swirl around Lou and his addiction, and now it's around Joey and his addiction. You might not know what a calm and healthy family looks like."

"I really don't. We really don't. Can you help us discover that and get us out of this crazy, addictive swirl? I don't want to pass this on to our grandchildren. I just want to be able to have everyone over for Rosh Hashanah, Yom Kippur, and Hanukah without it escalating into a fight."

"Do you remember the story in the Bible about Joseph?" I asked.

Defined by Wellness

If you or a family member is diagnosed with ADD, your family isn't automatically entered into the *dysfunctional* category—you just don't want the diagnosis to become your definition. You aren't defined by your disability. Or, as we prefer to say, you aren't defined by your *different-ness*. Your brain works differently than others, but that doesn't mean you are sentenced to lead a disordered and disappointing life. Your family should focus on wellness and health, not the diagnosis. The ideal center of your family is Christ. Your identity is in Him.

People with ADD contribute to a family or community with their high energy, spunk, resilience, creativity, persistence, and willingness to explore and take calculated risks. Later in this book, we'll see how some people have leveraged their ADD to perform at high levels in their respective industries. These positive traits are accompanied by the primary symptoms of ADD: distractibility, impulsivity, restlessness, and others. But the secondary symptoms are the ones that often cause the most damage.

These secondary symptoms develop because primary symptoms are not formally recognized. They include low self-esteem,

pioneer, expanding the frontiers of the tech world. He embodied Apple's slogan, "Think Different," a saying that perfectly sums up people who have ADD. He went places no one else could or would go in designing, building, and packaging products; he did things in ways that were incomprehensible to other people; and he introduced extraordinary ideas that were often dismissed until they revolutionized the industry. He carved out his own path, and in that sense, he also was an explorer.[2]

We admire someone with a sense of adventure and single-mindedness, someone with a passion to excel at the highest level, even against all odds. Olympians come to mind. In the 2016 Rio Olympics, we were inspired by world-class athletes who also have ADD: Michael Phelps in swimming, Justin Gatlin in track and field, Tim Howard in soccer, and Michelle Carter in shot-putting.

Many professional athletes have ADD. In fact, an estimated 8 to 10 percent of all pro athletes have the condition, compared to just 4 to 5 percent of the general adult population.[3]

As one of the top shot-putters in the world, Michelle Carter, a two-time Olympian and seven-time US champion, is currently ranked number one in the United States and number three in the world. She calls herself "Shot Diva" and likes to encourage others with attention issues: "I tell them you can do whatever you set your mind to—you just may do it differently. You may have to work a little bit harder, but you can do it."

Michael Phelps is the most decorated Olympian in history, ending his luminary career in Rio in 2016 at the age of thirty-one, winning five gold medals and a silver there to total twenty-eight medals. Doctors diagnosed him with ADD as a young child, and

Phelps found swimming to be an effective outlet for his abundant energy.

Justin Gatlin, Olympian track star and former world record holder in the one hundred meters, at 9.77 seconds, says, "Nothing could stop me—not even ADD." Gatlin says his condition fueled his love for track: "Ever since I could walk, I have been running. In class, I had trouble concentrating, but racing helped me focus."

Tim Howard, Olympic goalkeeper for the United States, says that his ADD helps him guard the goal because of the bursts of energy he gets and his ability to hyperfocus and block out other distractions. He has leveraged his ADD into a decorated professional career with the Colorado Rapids. ADD can be an asset if it is managed and the energy is directed toward a goal, like it is in athletics.

In addition to champion athletes, there are many accomplished musicians and actors with ADD whose diagnosis didn't limit their success. For instance, Adam Levine—the front man of Grammy Award–winning recording artists Maroon 5 and longtime coach on the NBC hit series *The Voice*—has ADHD. He explained, "When I was diagnosed with ADHD in my early teens, it was really helpful for me to learn that it was a real medical condition—I had ADHD. Now as an adult, I've worked with professionals to come up with a treatment plan that works for me. I like to remind young adults and adults that ADHD isn't a bad thing and that they shouldn't feel any different than others without ADHD. Always remember there are others going through the same thing."[4]

Other musicians like P!nk and will.i.am have been candid and "kept it real" about their ADD. To them, their music is therapeutic. Sometimes there is a stigma around ADD, but some of the most

successful artists in the world have this distinct
Gosling has leveraged his ADD into a successful
and actress Zooey Deschanel shared on her blog *HelloGiggles* ...
she has ADD and that "she loves to do easy crafts because they help
her focus on projects that can be completed very quickly."[5] In an
interview with *Cosmo*, actress Michelle Rodriguez revealed that she
has ADHD and sometimes has trouble focusing but has discovered
ways to make it work for her.[6]

Justin Timberlake was diagnosed with ADD as a child. Recently,
he told *ADDitude Magazine*, "If you're a young person called weird
or different [because you have ADD], I'm here to tell you that your
critics do not count. Their words will fade. You will not."[7]

The Entrepreneurial Edge

What do business mogul Sir Richard Branson, Ikea founder Ing-
var Kamprad, JetBlue founder David Neeleman, and Bill Gates
all have in common? Besides being monumentally successful
entrepreneurs and billionaires, they all have ADD, and like other
CEOs and entrepreneurs, some will tell you that they are successful largely *because* of their "diagnosis," not despite it.

The most common characteristics of ADD—creativity, multitasking, risk-taking, high energy, and resilience—are strengths
when leveraged in the right way and in the right career. It's why
so many high-profile achievers are beginning to publicly embrace
their diagnoses of ADD. People with ADD are often at their best
in crisis mode, multitasking and free associating to intuitively
reach a solution. And if they find something they truly love to do,
they are able to focus for hours on end.[8]

David Neeleman recently launched another successful airline, Azul in Brazil, pointing to another characteristic of ADD—resilience. He said, "If someone told me you could be normal or you could continue to have your ADD, I would take ADD. I can distill complicated facts and come up with simple solutions. I can look out on an industry with all kinds of problems and say, 'How can I do this better?' My ADD brain naturally searches for better ways of doing things."[9]

Neeleman continued, "Sometimes things happen in your career and in your life that you think at the time is devastating, and you wonder how you can recover, and you wonder how you are ever going to be able to turn it around. And a lot of times it is not *what happens to you in life, it is how you react to it.* I really believe that."[10]

Facing numerous challenges, roadblocks, and failures, Neeleman pressed on in the face of adversity, demonstrating an important element of resiliency—bounce. His reaction to difficulty was *How can I bounce back from this?*

This innate sense of optimism and hope about the future is common in successful entrepreneurs, especially those with ADD. They have the ability to recalibrate after a setback. Instead of giving up, their minds quickly shift to *What comes next?* Neeleman, Branson, Gates, and Kamprad all faced adversity—initially at school and later as they attempted to launch their innovative businesses—but each bounced back, making them the "comeback kids" of the ADD club.

There is an explanation for the resiliency and hope we see in successful entrepreneurs with ADD. Researchers have found some neurological and genetic commonalities. One recent UK study found a genetic link between a dopamine receptor gene variation associated with ADD and the tendency to be an entrepreneur. Sensation seeking, frequently observed in people with ADD, is more common among entrepreneurs than among the general population, and adult people with ADD are three times more likely to own or start their own businesses.[11]

It seems logical. Those with ADD are easily bored with routine, are quick to challenge the status quo, and tend to thrive in times of crisis. According to Dr. Dale Archer, "Those with ADHD in prehistoric times were constantly looking for new hunting grounds, water supplies and sites for a new place to settle. Village life made them restless, so they felt the urge to keep moving. In fact the gene associated with ADHD is sometimes called the 'explorer gene.' It takes an adventurous spirit to strike out on your own. Entrepreneurship fits perfectly with the ADHD'rs need for stimulation and a willingness to take risks."[12]

Radio host and former psychotherapist Thom Hartmann describes a person with ADD as "a hunter in a farmer's world." He explains how early humans were hunter-gatherers until they became agrarian and more sedentary. While the rest of humankind adapted to a farming culture, those with ADD retained some of the nomadic hunter-gatherer tendencies. Their explorer gene was at work with their preference to be active and their ability to hyperfocus, take calculated risks, and process complex information very quickly.[13]

In other words, the genetic material associated with high-energy, risk-taking, and boredom-averting behavior has contributed to the survival of the species. I know some parents and teachers would disagree, but humanity really does need people with ADD.

Researchers from several universities and private companies are currently investigating the explorer gene. Scientists from the University of California, Irvine, studied the genetic makeup of 2,320 individuals from thirty-nine different populations across the globe, including the Cheyenne tribe of North America, the Han of China, and the Mbuti of Africa. As they studied the migration patterns of these groups (dating back to early humans), they discovered a predominance of a genetic commonality—what came to be known as *7R*. This variant is a "long allele of the dopamine transporter gene—a variant of the D4 receptor gene called 7R and is linked with ADD and is now commonly referred to as the *explorer gene.*"[14]

Ancient humans needed both the explorer and the settler to survive. When times were good and the living was easy, the settler mind-set benefitted the group, keeping things predictable and stable. But when challenging times arose and resources were limited, the group needed the explorers, the risk-takers, and the adventurers to step up and challenge the status quo and discover new resources or move the tribe to a safer region.

CHAPTER FOUR

Hi, My Name Is Pat, and I'm ... Is There More Coffee?

We are curious about how people with attention deficit disorder (ADD) organize themselves. Some use a method like my client Pat. What follows is a conversation I had with her.

"You should see my house. I have piles by the door, piles on the kitchen counter, piles on the stairs to remind me to take them upstairs, and stuff at the top of the stairs to remind me to take them downstairs," confessed Pat, a forty-four-year-old single mom. "Piles of dirty and clean clothes on my bedroom floor and down the hall—toward the laundry room. The sink is filled to the brim with piles of plates and dirty pots, and I think right now the trash is piled up and probably spilling out to where the dog can get into it. My life is a bunch of piles!"

"How long has it been this way?" I asked.

"Since I was a kid. My ex used to call them 'Patty's piles.' That's why he's my ex. I don't like being called 'Patty,' and I don't like him putting down my organizational methods." A slight smile came across her face, calling attention to her carefully applied lipstick. She took a sip of water and continued, "It starts out as a way to organize. I'm visual, so if I can see it, I'm more likely to remember it, so I spread reminders all over the house. It works at first, but then it gets out of control. I'll discover a clear horizontal space and I think, *This space needs a new pile.* And I'll put something there. *It's just there temporarily,* I tell myself. After a while, I'll think that the pile looks small or lonely, so I add something to it. Typically, the things I add are unrelated to the content of the original pile. Now my purposeful pile is messed up because its purpose is fuzzy. I might have computer cords mixed in with solo socks. What originally made sense organizationally doesn't make sense now."

"So what do you do?"

"I just ignore the piles. I walk around them until I'm forced to find something. Most of the time, I just go buy whatever I can't find, and 90 percent of the time, I'll find what I was looking for within twenty-four hours of buying a replacement. It's frustrating and expensive!"

"Do you return the replacement item to the store?"

"No, because I can't find the receipt in my pile of receipts."

"So what do you do with the extra item?"

"I put it in a pile."

This is humorous, unless you have to live with it—either as the "piler" or as a spouse or child of the piler. But there is hope. We have a lot of experience in support groups for recovery. We've always liked the concept of a group for people with ADD—like a twelve-step group where people can admit their ADD in a safe setting: "Hi, my name is Pat and I'm ... is there more coffee?"

But we're not sure it would work. People with ADD might get distracted, be late, get sidetracked in sharing, or impulsively interrupt each other. Still, those with ADD could use some understanding, support, and practical tips on how to manage their ADD instead of it managing them. There is help for the perpetually distracted; there is relief for the perpetual piler.

Factors That Don't Help ADD

ADD, like other challenges, worsens when stress enters the equation. Having your annual performance review at work might make your ADD more intense the week before and after your evaluation. Any disruption to your schedule or routine can ramp up your ADD—a change in your job, school, residence, and home life, to name a few. Parents of newborns often suffer from sleep deprivation, which can make ADD symptoms more severe.

A lack of nutritious and unprocessed food can also affect your condition. Swinging through the drive-through and grabbing the combo meal for breakfast is easy but might work against you a few hours later when it comes time to focus, be still, or listen.

If you have ADD, having a jam-packed schedule might seem to work for you. After all, you have the energy for it. You can plan on twelve- and fourteen-hour days, but you might not be working efficiently. Take time to reflect, think, prioritize, and schedule gaps in your day. In those gaps, take a few minutes to congratulate yourself for what you've accomplished and then ask yourself, *Is what I'm planning to do next the most important or the most urgent?* It might seem urgent, but unless there's a deadline, you might be able to do it later and focus on something else that's pressing.

It's been our observation that adults with ADD move fast and long, but many of them waste energy, get sidetracked, lose things, have to repeat tasks because they were done sloppily, or don't have the resources or time to complete tasks because they didn't plan effectively. Taking time to pause for "props and planning" is our suggestion. *Props* is slang for "propping someone up with a compliment." In this case, you are propping yourself. If you have ADD, take time for "props and planning" three to five times a day versus rushing from task to task. You will probably work smarter and be more rested at the end of the day.

In this chapter, we will look at different kinds of ADD, how males and females with ADD differ, how ADD affects brain function, and what healthy habits can enhance cognitive functioning in those with ADD. Doctors, therapists, and even teachers and parents who understand ADD and its particular types can address it more effectively.

Different Kinds of ADD

Not too long ago, when parents first noticed features or traits of ADD in a preschool child, the child might be labeled "active." A few years later, teachers might call that student "restless" or "disruptive" or "distracted" and take disciplinary action.

Teachers often carried out this kind of discipline in front of the entire class. Educators saw ADD as a behavior or character issue—primarily with boys; they believed ADD did not affect girls. We know now that this is false, although girls with ADD might not display symptoms in the same ways as boys with ADD.

felt the same. The findings indicate that very few females or males report feeling worse after being diagnosed with ADD. Once again, we encourage an early diagnosis so that teens and young adults don't struggle with low self-esteem and the fallout of experiencing second-ary symptoms of ADD as adults.

Experts in the field are conducting research on diagnostic cri-terion based on gender. Perhaps the next edition of the *DSM* will provide gender-specific diagnoses.

We have seen that ADD can't be accurately addressed with a "one-size-fits-all" label. There are differences between genders and among factors of hyperactivity, inattention, and impulse control.

Therefore, the restrictive criterion of the *DSM-5* could use some work. We prefer instead using current technology to more accu-rately diagnose the various kinds of ADD. Typically, a medical doctor, psychiatrist, psychologist, or licensed therapist diagnoses ADD. Most use a list of diagnostic questions that they ask the patient. Teachers and parents usually provide input for young chil-dren. This is the most common form of diagnosis.

But what if there was a way to actually *see* what's going on in the mind of a person with ADD?

With brain imaging, we can observe the brain at work and see various areas of the brain that are associated with ADD. Single-photon emission computed tomography (SPECT) imaging is a sophisticated brain imaging tool. Trained doctors can observe a brain and determine the areas affected by ADD by combining SPECT imaging with a quantitative electroencephalogram (EEG) to measure the electrical activity of the brain.

Dr. Daniel Amen, board-certified child, adolescent, and adult psychiatrist licensed in nuclear brain imaging, is a pioneer in this type of high-tech diagnosis. Dr. Amen has more than 120,000 SPECT scans from patients from 111 countries. He has discovered a cutting-edge approach to diagnose and treat ADD.

A person with ADD has a different brain than a person without ADD. It's a matter of biology and chemistry; they are wired differently.

Generally, when people without ADD concentrate, blood flow to the brain increases, especially in the prefrontal cortex. This increased activity allows us to focus, stay on task, and think ahead. In the brains of most people with ADD, blood flow to the brain decreases when they concentrate, making it difficult to stay focused. In other words, the harder they try, the harder it gets!

ADD, like many other conditions, is not just a single and simple disorder; therefore, there is no universal treatment. Dr. Amen has identified seven types of ADD, and each requires a different treatment plan because of the diverse brain systems involved.[2]

Seven Types of ADD[3]

Dr. Amen's excellent book *Healing ADD: The Breakthrough Program That Allows You to See and Heal the 7 Types of ADD* gives us a more specific categorization and diagnosis of someone with ADD. The goal of our book is to help the reader understand and love a person with ADD. You can be more empathetic when you understand these seven types:

1. **Classic ADD (ADHD).** People with this type tend to be inattentive, distractible, disorganized, hyperactive, restless, and impulsive.
2. **Inattentive ADD.** This type comprises people who are inattentive, easily distracted, disorganized, and often described as "space cadets," "daydreamers," or "couch potatoes." Not hyperactive!
3. **Overfocused ADD.** People with this type are inattentive, have trouble shifting attention, frequently get stuck in loops of negative thoughts or behaviors, are obsessive, worry excessively, are inflexible, and often display oppositional and argumentative behavior. Can be hyperactive.
4. **Temporal lobe ADD.** These people are inattentive, easily distracted, disorganized, and irritable. They can have a short fuse, dark thoughts, or mood instability. They might also struggle with learning disabilities. Can be hyperactive.
5. **Limbic ADD.** People with this kind of ADD are inattentive, easily distracted, and disorganized. They can experience chronic low-grade sadness or negativity, "glass-half-empty syndrome," and low energy and tend to be more isolated socially, with frequent feelings of hopelessness and worthlessness. Can be hyperactive.
6. **Ring-of-fire ADD.** People with this type are inattentive, easily distracted, irritable, overly sensitive, and oppositional, with cyclic moodiness. Can be hyperactive.
7. **Anxious ADD.** Inattentiveness, distractibility, disorganization, tension, nervousness, pessimism, test anxiety, and

social anxiety characterize this type. Sufferers also frequently develop physical responses to stress, such as headaches and gastrointestinal symptoms. Can be hyperactive.

You need to know the type of ADD you are dealing with to get the right help for yourself or your loved one. Brain imaging is a powerful resource for diagnosing specific kinds of ADD. It is possible to have more than one type. You can find out more about SPECT imaging at www.amenclinics.com.

We suggest to our readers a free and easy ADD type test available online at www.amenclinics.com/HealingADDtypetest.com.

The first step in addressing ADD for yourself or a loved one is determining if you actually have ADD. People first display symptoms of ADD in their developmental years; therefore, ADD is called a *developmental disorder*. It is not something that surprisingly appears midlife. If someone suddenly has ADD symptoms but never had them as a child, they are likely due to something else, such as anxiety, depression, chronic stress, hormonal changes, a head injury, substance abuse, or other forms of exposure to toxins.

We've observed six classic symptoms that typically point to ADD in our experience of working with numerous clients over the years.

Six Classic Symptoms of ADD

1. **Short attention span for everyday tasks.** Someone with ADD will become inattentive and need some form of excitement to stay engaged in mundane chores or activities.

2. **Distractibility.** People with ADD have heightened sensory awareness. They can see, smell, feel, hear, and touch things and be much more aware of one or more of these senses than a person without ADD. They are easily distracted by all this information as it streams into their brains.

3. **Disorganization.** People with ADD struggle to complete projects and tasks on time. They might not be able to find the necessary tools and resources for a job, often misplacing what they need and then losing time searching. They often demonstrate disorganization in the form of a messy work-space, computer desktop, laptop bag, bedroom, or car.

4. **Irritability.** Someone with ADD can become irritable or moody due to the frustration of losing things, being late, and sensing disappointment from spouses, friends, cowork-ers, and bosses. We often see men who are irritable, moody, or negative with undiagnosed ADD. They've been asked by their wives or girlfriends to "get some help."

5. **Impulsivity.** Many people with ADD have challenges with judgment and controlling their impulses. They often "go with their gut," but their gut is giving them inaccurate data. They might say or do things without thinking through the ramifications. They struggle making a causal connection. In

other words, they don't clearly see that their behavior and words have consequences—frequently negative ones.

6. **Procrastination.** Some people with ADD might have the motto "Why do today what you can put off until tomorrow?" They spend lots of energy stalling and avoiding, especially if it's a boring task. Some learn to wait until the last minute—right up against the deadline—because they "work better under pressure." Or they wait until someone is upset with their past-due performance and complains.

People without ADD might also demonstrate some of these traits, though not to the same extent. We've all been bored and inattentive. Most of us have some areas of disorganization in our lives. (To be ultraorganized is a different kind of problem.) We've all been irritated, impulsive, and stalled, but that doesn't mean we have ADD. But when a person exhibits these traits often and in intense ways, he or she might have ADD.

ADD on a Continuum

Each type of ADD is on a continuum. Someone might have classic ADD at a high level and temporal lobe ADD at a low level. Some doctors and therapists who specialize in ADD use a five- or ten-point scale to determine the severity of symptoms of ADD in their diagnosis. We prefer the ten-point continuum for accuracy, with 1 being *never* and 10 being *often or always* on the continuum.[4] For example, you might have inattentive ADD on a scale of 6, but you could have a child with classic ADD with hyperactivity at 8. In this case, doctors would develop an effective treatment strategy for your ADD that differs from your child's by addressing the type of ADD and the intensity of the symptoms.

The ADD continuum delineates where *typical* behavior ends and where something diagnosable and treatable begins. For example, a high-energy person could score in the midrange (4–6) on *activity*, but he or she does not have a disorder until he or she has a frenzied episode and symptoms interfere with everyday functioning. Someone who works sixteen hours a day; is a rapid, nonstop talker; gets five hours of sleep; doesn't complete tasks; and takes extreme risks—physically, financially, or relationally—likely has ADD.

However, someone on the high end of the continuum might be extremely adventurous, energetic, and different from the norm but still not need treatment. He or she simply leverages the ADD in a way that works for him or her. (Think Richard Branson, Michael Jordan, and Karina Smirnoff.)

Getting Help for ADD

Of course, not everyone is a Richard Branson or Michael Jordan. Instead of designing a career to maximize our unique strengths and minimize the liabilities of ADD, we might need some type of treatment. We like what Dr. Patricia Quinn, M.D., a developmental pediatrician and expert on ADD, said in an interview: "I'm not the sort of person who thinks ADD is a strength, but I do think you can use it to become successful."[5]

Nohl did well in high school and was accepted into a top-tier university's nationally acclaimed theoretical math major. His family physician diagnosed him with ADD in middle school, and

Nohl had been taking medication ever since. Listen in to our conversation at a recent session.

"When I need to catch up on my homework or take a big exam, I double-up on my dosage. It works very well as a 'study drug,'" Nohl told me as he sat in my office. He wore shorts, flip-flops, and a T-shirt with his fraternity letters on it. "Everything worked well until guys in my house wanted some, so I sold it to them. It made me popular. I desperately wanted to be cool and have friends. This worked my sophomore and junior years, but then I ran out and couldn't get more. I had sold it all. At a party, I drank too much and impulsively said some stupid things to the president of my frat. One of my brothers from the house took offense and called me a name. I called him out, and the next thing I knew, we were fighting. I was too drunk to deliver my punches quickly. I'm sure I looked like a drunken idiot, flailing with my fists. I wound up in the back of an ambulance with a bloody nose, black eye, cut lip, and concussion I got when I hit the floor after he knocked me out with a hook."

"Wow, that sounds terrible. What happened?" I asked.

"They took me to the hospital and stitched me up. I was too embarrassed to go back to the frat house, so I went home to my parents' house. When I got back to the frat house, I found out that everyone had met on Sunday and took a vote—they suspended my membership from the fraternity the first quarter of my senior year! I was angry and devastated."

"What did you do?"

"I got drunk at a bar downtown. My life was worthless. I finally had friends, and now they rejected me. I couldn't study. I had to move out of the house by the end of the quarter. All my *brothers* acted like I was contagious. When I saw them, they turned away. They didn't return my texts. I'd say hi to them at the house or on campus, and they'd give me the stink-eye as if to say, 'Why are *you* talking to us?' It was painful. I moved into an apartment on campus and partied. I had a difficult time going to class, let alone doing the work."

"So what's your status now with the university?"

"I'm on probation. I have to raise my grades from failing to a 2.0 or get kicked out of the program—which means out of the university. That's why I'm here. My parents told me I had to meet with you. Can you help me?"

"Yes, I can. It's going to take some significant changes, but if you make them, you will be healthier, and you can possibly stay in school. Are you up for the challenge?"

"Yeah, I worked too hard to bail on this."

"Okay, let's do this. People with ADD often develop thoughts and scripts that they run through their head: 'I'm a failure. I can't pay attention. I'm weird,' or 'Everyone is looking at me.' These thoughts limit your ability to have fun and study or work effectively. Constant self-doubt tends to rule your mind. Sound familiar?"

"Yeah, it's like you're reading my mind."

"In contrast, hopeful and positive thoughts tend to generate a sense of capability, confidence, and achievement. Both negative and positive thoughts have corresponding scripts or MP3 recordings we play in our heads. What are some of yours?"

"'I'm always messing things up,' 'I don't belong,' and 'I'll never have a girlfriend.'"

"We call those scripts, and the corresponding thoughts ANTs—automatic negative thoughts. These typically come from things others have told us—maybe a teacher, coach, or parent."

"I got it from all three."

"Well, that would do it. Unfortunately, as a kid or teen, nobody teaches you to filter and process that stuff. You don't know how to challenge your thoughts or process your feelings. We spend time learning the capitals of every state, but we don't learn how to think clearly. As a result, our pesky ANTs can make us anxious, depressed, and distracted."

"I'm all three—and I'm angry. It doesn't take much to set me off," admitted Nohl as he kicked off his flip-flops and crossed his legs. "So how do I kill these ANTs?"

"This warped thinking process is called cognitive distortion. Cognitive distortions are errors in the way we think. They are familiar. We practice them dozens of times a day, but they are distorted, off. And if our thinking is off, even by 15 percent from reality, our feelings are going to be off. Instead of feeling happy, capable, and content, we are more likely to feel depressed, worthless, and discontented. Some people, like you, get tired of feeling this way and want to pin it on someone, so they get angry. People with cognitive distortions, or ANTs, stay angry 24-7."[6]

"That's me, absolutely! So what do I do?"

"You took biology and chemistry, right?"

"Yeah, and I also took a neuroscience class."

"Perfect. So you know that every time you have a thought, your brain releases chemicals. An electrical transmission crosses your brain, and you become aware of what you are thinking.

Every time you get angry or depressed, your brain releases chemicals that make your body feel bad. Your muscles might get tense, your heart beats faster, your hands get sweaty, and you might get the sense to fight, flight, or freeze."

"Exactly."

"In contrast, every time you have a positive, hopeful, or kind thought, your brain releases chemicals that make your body feel good. Think about a time when you got a good grade on a test, a friend gave you a compliment, or you cuddled with your dog. You feel good, right? When you are happy, your muscles relax, you feel calm, your heart rate and breathing are slower, and your hands aren't sweaty. Your body reacts to both distorted thoughts—which tend to be negative—and positive and accurate thoughts. Your body reacts to every thought you have, influencing your emotions. Our thoughts are powerful. They can make us feel healthy, strong, and calm. Your thoughts affect your body at a cellular level. So we need to be aware of our 'automatic' thoughts. If we don't pay attention to them, they become a toxic habit. Your thoughts do not always tell the truth. That's why we call them cognitive distortions. Here is a list of ten of them. Which of these ANTs do you practice?"

Nohl quickly read the list. "Nine out of the ten."

"No wonder you feel so bad." I smiled sympathetically at him.

"No doubt." He laughed. "I've been doing these nine since I was in middle school."

"And because you are smart, you can process a lot of content quicker than an average student. You might have been processing ANTs at lightning speed because of your broadband brain, with the result of feeling pretty bad."

"All the time."

"Here's the key: you don't have to believe every thought that goes through your head. I know your university; they teach you to be analytical, maybe even a little skeptical. That's what I want you to do with your thoughts. Think about your thoughts—we call it metacognition. When you have a thought that seems a little biased or off, call it out. Say to yourself, or even out loud, 'ANT!'"

He laughed. "They'd really think I'm crazy if I did that."

"Actually, you'll be less 'crazy' if you do. You'll be less reactive and calmer, and you'll be able to think with clarity. ANTs are happiness-suckers. Once you identify them, call them out, and replace them with accurate and positive self-scripts, you are likely to feel better."

"How do I do that? My default is distracted, reactive, and pessimistic."

"Start there. Admit that you want to change those distortions and their corresponding negative scripts. If you never challenge your thoughts, you just believe them as if they were true. It's up to you to change how you program your mind."

"How do I do that? I need to change my thinking and how I feel or I'm going to be kicked out of school."

"Whenever you notice an ANT crossing your mind, call out 'ANT' and write it down. Record it in your phone's notes. Which one of these ten cognitive distortions is it? Then write down your negative script, which might have become automatic by now. Third, write down a positive script to replace the negative one and rehearse it in your mind for a few seconds. You're replacing toxic

input with healthy and undistorted input. Garba
out—it's basic programming."

"It's easier to do on a computer."

"You are right."

Nohl began working on killing his ANTs and started feeling better
about himself. His new self-confidence and positivity generated
a sliver of hope that helped him dig his way out of his depression and academic hole. He learned how to leverage his hyperfocus superpowers from ADD with his studies, alternating short,
focused study periods with five minutes of push-ups or planks. He
raised his grades and stayed in college.

This is an example of cognitive behavioral therapy (CBT) at
work. Professionals who use CBT have shown that it is effective
in treating ADD, anxiety, depression, and other issues. It is especially useful when the professional helps the client discover new
ways of thinking and new habits of behavior. Most people with
ADD need structure and life skills to improve their lives. They
need new habits. Some ADD coaches combine CBT with a more
directive behavior therapy to help build structure, accountability,
and rewards into the lives of their clients.

If you learn about these various issues of ADD, understanding
and loving yourself or someone with the condition will be easier.

CHAPTER FIVE

Five Qualities of a Healthy Relationship (with Someone with ADD)

I warmed myself in the autumn sun of southwestern Pennsylvania. It was colder than the weather I was accustomed to in Southern California, and I had left my jacket in my room. The sun felt good on my face. I had just finished a session with fathers and sons on the topic "Keys to a Healthy Family." I have the privilege of being a resource person for Young Presidents' Organization (YPO), and I was spending the weekend at a comfortable resort and former hunting lodge.

I sat on the bench at the field club and watched the dads and sons shoot shotguns at sporting clays. I could see the delight on the boys' faces when they hit their target.

"Excuse me, sorry to bother you, but can I ask you a question?" asked Brian, one of the dads at the retreat.

"Sure, I'm just sitting here watching. Did you shoot already?"

"Yes, and that's my son, Blake, up there. He's watching his friend. Are you sure it's okay to ask you a quick question?" He looked over both of his shoulders.

"Of course."

"Great. I liked what you had to say about healthy families. Blake and I are going to work on those qualities you went over this morning, but I have one problem."

"What's that?"

"I am an entrepreneur, just like most of the dads here. There are a lot of entrepreneurs in YPO. We like to start things. We like the thrill of something new, something we created. My company has done very well since I started it out of college. I can lead thousands of employees as CEO, but it's difficult to lead at home. I have ADD, and I can focus at work on the stuff I'm interested in and delegate the rest, but I can't delegate my responsibilities at home. How do I deal with my ADD and be more attentive to my wife and kids?"

I gave Brian a quick response and suggested we talk more after the retreat. He joined his son, and I moved over to another group of dads and sons at the archery range. I wasn't interested in shooting arrows, so I sat on a picnic table and watched the sons and dads shoot. I observed that there were fewer people here than at the shotgun range, but they were having fun, and it was a lot quieter.

After a few minutes, another father named Clarke approached me. "Hey, can I bother you?" he asked. "My son is in line for archery, and I wanted to ask you a private question. May I?"

"Absolutely! Join me." I patted the tabletop, and he joined me there—our feet on the bench, the sun at our backs, and our gazes fixed on the boys shooting.

"I like what I've heard so far and am looking forward to our next session. I really want my family to be healthy. I didn't grow up in a healthy family, so I don't have a best practice in mind. As a leader and founder of my company, I can lead at work. I like to dream, cast vision, and develop clarity around our core values, but I have no clue on how to do that at home. I feel fulfilled at work and unsuccessful at home. My wife and I aren't on the same page. Is that very common?" He looked around to make sure no one could hear us.

"It's more common than you think. We can learn business leadership skills at college. We can enroll in an MBA program and be a hero at work, but most of us haven't taken the time to get our master's in family leadership."

"My wife says I need to bring some of my leadership skills to leading our family, but when I get home, I forget and keep busy running the kids to practice, rehearsals, games, and other activities. She says I lack follow-through at home."

"Have you ever been diagnosed with ADD?"

Clarke looked somewhat puzzled. "Yeah ... well ... why do you ask that?"

"A lot of successful entrepreneurs have ADD. We can see it with a lot of the dads here at the retreat this weekend. The risk-taking, the thrill of starting your own business, the energy, and the out-of-the-box thinking are all traits of ADD."

"I just wanted to get out of my boring stockbroker job, so I launched my own company. What does ADD have to do with it?"

"You can hyperfocus at work because you are in the zone, interested in what you are doing, and have a passion and aptitude for it—plus, you get paid. At home, you are likely not in a zone of flow, you might not be fully engaged in what you are doing, and you aren't getting paid for it. At home, you are more likely to lack the follow-through. Has your wife mentioned that?"

"Every weekend!" he laughed. "She begins Friday with 'What will you do for me this weekend that I asked for previously?' If I performed like this at work, I'd fire myself!"

Several other dads privately approached me that weekend, each sharing a similar story of success at work but distraction and a lack of clarity and follow-through at home.

One confided that his wife was upset with his impulsive spending habits, which she said were "spoiling the kids." Another dad told me that he had procrastinated signing up for the retreat for three years, but with his wife's "nagging," he finally did it. "I don't know why I procrastinate. My son is thirteen and the oldest kid here; we could have been here when he was ten."

As I said earlier, there are many examples of successful entrepreneurs who have ADD. The fathers I met at this retreat wanted a healthier home. Many of them told me they had ADD, but it hadn't kept them from success at work. Now they wanted success at home.

Five Qualities of a Healthy Home

Search Institute researchers have studied key developmental assets for adolescents for several years. They determined forty assets for capable teens and delivered strategies to schools, parents, and youth groups on how to become an asset-building community.[1] The researchers spent years developing these assets with teens and then realized that sending these kids home to a family system that might not support their recently acquired skills wasn't a good model.

Researchers sought to determine the common competencies and characteristics of a healthy home. Their investigation became known as *The American Family Assets Study.*[2] The researchers determined twenty-one habits that the healthiest families have in common. These habits are categorized under five key components of a balanced and healthy home that is more likely to produce capable, high-achieving family members—both adults and children.

The study of more than 1,511 families reflects a representative population based on the US Census, with families with at least one child, age ten to fifteen. The sample is a representative population of urban, suburban, and rural families across all sectors: socioeconomic, ethnic, racial, gender, marital status, sexual orientation, and religious or nonreligious status.[3]

If you have ADD, look for ways to enhance these five qualities in small ways in your personal and family life. If you live with someone with ADD, have a discussion on how you could work together to strengthen these five qualities.

1. Nurturing Relationships

Healthy families exhibit nurturing relationships. Besides encouraging each other and being open and authentic, these families also demonstrate affection and positive communication. For the family with an adult with ADD, positive communication is critical. Instead of negative, impulsive, or critical communication, healthy families have members who listen attentively and speak respectfully to each other.

Words matter. They aren't neutral—the

subtracting from someone's life. Words ge

spoke life into existence with just a word (

Impulsive, reactionary speech can be

appropriate word at the right time brings

the reckless pierce like swords, but the tongue of the wise brings

healing" (Prov. 12:18).

Healthy homes use words to build: "Do not let any *unwhole-some* talk come out of your mouths, but only what is helpful for building others up according to their needs, that it may benefit those who listen" (Eph. 4:29). We don't use the word *unwholesome* too much these days, but you might have heard its antonym used in old movies from the sixties. *Wholesome* means "good," "clean," and "without anything bad." In Ephesians, *unwholesome* is the Greek word *sapros*, which means "corrupt," "tainted," or "toxic."

If you live with someone with ADD, you really need your words to be pure and positive, not laced with negative or critical words. A person with ADD often remembers hurtful or critical comments from friends, parents, teachers, or bosses. He or she can feel "less than" when reflecting on these toxic words. A person with ADD can understand and be understood when we use positive and clear communication. Understanding needs to flow both ways.

People with ADD can be very reactive to negatively charged words. People with ADD tend to be a rebellious group. They don't like being corrected or told what to do. They are comfortable making others uncomfortable. They question everything and can become irritable or argumentative when a family member comes across as an authority figure. If people with ADD are told what to heir knee-jerk reaction might be to defiantly do the opposite. t's not always intentional or conscious; it's just one of the many ways adults with ADD are wired differently.

Criticism tends to make things worse for adults with ADD. Instead, they need accepting and supportive words. People we love need our encouragement. They need to be accepted and supported—especially those with ADD.

One of our tips for positive communication is to switch a negative to a positive. Change a criticism to a request. Instead of "Why can't you ever pick up after yourself?" say "I really feel a sense of calm when I come into the kitchen and see that you've put things where they belong. I appreciate it when you do that. Thanks. Do you think you could start doing that most of the time?"

2. Established Routines

Adults with ADD need some structure in the home and in the rhythm of family life to function well. They bring the *fun* to *function*, but they do need some order to direct them. You can establish routines most effectively when you engage the adult with ADD in the process—*with* the person with ADD versus *for* the person with ADD. The adult with ADD wants to be respected as an adult, not treated like a child.

People commonly describe adults with ADD as immature or childish. People don't know how else to make sense of this kind of behavior, so they attack it as being beneath adult standards. They hope to shame the person into changing his or her ways, but that tactic usually doesn't work.[4]

Adults with ADD are easily distracted, so adding a natural rhythm to their home life adds order and a sense of predictability. Much like the tides of the ocean—ebbing and flowing four times a day—a person with ADD needs consistency, without restraints. There's enough order to plan on the tide coming up or going down but not too much order that it gets in the way of life.

Healthy families develop intentional structure—especially families with an adult with ADD. The four most common established routines of healthy families follow:

1. **Family meals.** Family members eat meals together most days of a typical week.
2. **Shared activities.** Family members regularly spend time doing everyday activities together.
3. **Meaningful traditions.** Holidays, rituals, and celebrations are part of family life.
4. **Dependability.** Family members know what to expect from one another each day.

Looking forward to these traditions and routines adds structure to family life without rigidity. Researchers at the Search Institute found that more intentional structure and predictability in families is needed.[5] Only 27 percent of the sample families reported that they were consistent. This means that 73 percent of families describe themselves as inconsistent. Consistency breeds security, trust, connection, humor, and commitment in families. Children learn that "I can depend on Dad because he picks me up on time" and "I look forward to Friday pizza night because my mom lets me choose the pizza and my sister gets to choose the movie."

Healthy routines enhance consistency. In a family with an adult with ADD, consistency can be lacking. Doubt, suspicion, and cynicism might grow in the vacuum. Families that share meals, chores, activities, and traditions create a sense of camaraderie and provide just enough order and connection without becoming cumbersome.

Relationships, particularly marriage, take work. For the partner with ADD, relationships can be especially challenging. His partner might misinterpret his forgetfulness as a lack of interest. Her partner might get resentful when he has to pick up the slack for mundane chores and childcare.

Melissa Orlov, author of *The ADHD Effect on Marriage*, reports that the divorce rate is nearly twice as high for people with ADD than for those without the condition.[6] It has been our experience that anger, resentment, criticism, and blaming are the relationship-killers for couples. If the non-ADD spouse is feeling devalued, forgotten, or taken advantage of, these toxic habits tend to prevail, and the seeds of divorce are planted.

Families with an adult with ADD need consistency. They need what the Bible calls "self-control." Thankfully, we don't have to generate this ourselves. God gave believers His Holy Spirit, and one of the evidences (fruits) of God's Spirit is self-control: "But the fruit of the Spirit is love, joy, peace, forbearance, kindness, goodness, faithfulness, gentleness and *self-control*. Against such things there is no law" (Gal. 5:22–23, emphasis added).

Our divine resource and basis for consistency is self-control, as a fruit of the Spirit. A person with ADD can admit, "I don't have what it takes, but the Holy Spirit does." In this case, self-control is the ability to set a course and stick to it. When a Christ-follower cooperates with God's Spirit, he or she notices a difference: "And do not grieve the Holy Spirit of God, with whom you were sealed for the day of redemption. Get rid of all bitterness, rage and anger, brawling and slander, along with every form of malice. Be kind and compassionate to one another, forgiving each other, just as in Christ God forgave you" (Eph. 4:30–32).

An adult with ADD needs God to help him or her with self-control. Someone married to or in relationship with an adult with ADD also needs an extralarge serving of self-control. When we try to handle these challenges in our own strength, we tend to mess it up. When we deny God's power (which is readily available within us), we grieve God's Spirit. His desire is for us to cooperate with Him, to yield our stubborn will to Him. When we do this, we experience self-control and other fruits of the Spirit. When we grieve the Holy Spirit by seeking to handle things on our own, we kill the process of consistency that is developing within us.

We can move from *react* to *respond* with God's help. Reacting in an ADD relationship produces more drama, while responding leads to kindness, compassion, and forgiveness: "Everyone should be quick to listen, slow to speak and slow to become angry, because human anger does not produce the righteousness that God desires" (James 1:19–20).

We like to ask our ADD clients where they feel they could use more self-control. Self-control is about movement. At times, you need self-control to get out of bed and get moving. At other times, you need it to slow down and stop. Self-control helps us regulate our speed and what we do and say. As we ask our clients with ADD, "With self-control, do you need the start or the stop?"

3. Realistic Expectations

We noticed that couples where one or both partners has ADD can easily fall into a vicious cycle that author Melissa Orlov calls "symptom-response-response." The so-called symptoms of ADD aren't necessarily the problem so much as how the non-ADD spouse reacts to them.[7] Let's say that you are the person without ADD, and you are looking forward to sharing exciting news from work with your ADD husband. You begin sharing, and you notice that he isn't fully present and is thinking about something else. You could react by asking, "Why aren't you listening to me?" which would likely generate the reaction, "Why are you yelling at me?"

Or you could respond when you observe a symptom of ADD, like distractibility: "I could really use your full attention right now. I will be brief." Move toward him, sit on the couch, and reach for his hand. Gain his eye contact and say, "Thanks, I appreciate you giving me your undivided attention. I'll keep this short." Then summarize the information into essential bullet points with no side stories or tangents (those could be rabbit trails that take you off-topic).

This is one form of establishing realistic expectations for couples. Don't expect your ADD husband to be able to chat away for thirty minutes like you would expect with your best friend. Think bullet points, executive summary, highlights, essentials, and other punctuated bits of content. He's more likely to engage, listen, and understand you. And you will feel more valued and connected.

Here are six positive pointers for establishing realistic expectations for couples in ADD relationships:

1. **Remember why you love this person.** What first attracted you to him or her? Was it his spontaneity? Her energy or enthusiasm or willingness to take risks? Maintaining your relationship is like maintaining a road. It isn't that exciting, but it's crucial. It's easy to let the maintenance—the parenting, the scheduling, the planning, and paying bills—overshadow the attraction, the romance, and the passion you had before your relationship became so chaotic. Rediscover the allure.

2. **Be patient.** Most adults with ADD have experienced parents, teachers, coaches, coworkers, and bosses who have been exasperated with them and lost their patience. Your spouse with ADD needs your patience or she might react defensively, expecting to be blamed for everything. Be very clear that your role is not to be the critical parent but to be on his team in a supportive role. We like to use the analogy of a NASCAR pit crew. Not everyone is driving the car, but when the car pulls in for a pit stop, everyone snaps into action to get the car back out on the track as quickly as possible. Most of the race, they are watching, being patient, and listening to the driver give them information about the car's performance. A stellar pit crew is patient, knows its job, and jumps into action when needed. Your ADD spouse needs this kind of support and help (without enabling).

3. **Set aside time to connect.** Relationships can't grow at microwave speed. They need to slowly simmer like food in a Crock-Pot. People with ADD can be so addicted to adrenaline, they fill their day with their agenda and leave no gaps for unexpected tasks or time to relax, play, talk, and be romantic with their spouses. If you are the one with ADD, realize that it affects your spouse's life and your relationship. Take time to process, listen, understand, and connect. You don't always need to solve problems during these times of connection. Connect first, direct second.

4. **Empathize.** As you listen and "feel with" your spouse, you will increase your understanding. We like to tell couples that understanding does not equal agreement. We will often write the following equation on a whiteboard:

Understanding ≠ Agreement

We want couples to take time to empathize and understand but not necessarily resolve issues, compromise, and work toward alignment or agreement. We've observed that couples who empathize have higher trust and resolve problems quickly, or they decide not to "sweat the small stuff" and let petty issues go. Why? Because they are more committed to the relationship than being right.

5. **Determine baby steps together.** Decide together small, incremental steps each person can take. Don't create unrealistic goals or push for too much change—it will backfire with an adult with ADD. It's not about working harder; it's about working smarter. It's the principle of the *slight*

edge—making small, incremental changes over time. They are barely noticeable day to day: no one will notice if you do it or don't do it today, but over time, they have an incremental impact that compounds. Record in writing the baby steps that each of you will take and celebrate *wins* at the end of the day or several times a week. An example of a couple's baby steps might look like this:

- Wanda Wife (does not have ADD) will buy bread and lunch meat for her husband when she does weekly grocery shopping.
- Harry Husband (has ADD) will set a daily alarm on workdays at 9:00 p.m. to remind him to make his lunch, set the timer for coffee, and place a sticky note on the coffeemaker that says "Lunch in fridge" to remind him to take it out and set it by the front door.

6. **Be partners.** Don't blame each other or set up your spouse for failure. If there is an issue or a "fail," use it as an opportunity to discuss, learn, and reset with a fresh strategy of baby steps. Don't hold out for changing your ADD spouse in an area that isn't his or her strength. For instance, don't expect your spouse to organize the garage and label where everything goes if he or she has ADD. Do it together or hire an organizer to help you. Set each other up for success. Be modest with your growth goals but overcelebrate each step forward. Be very clear about household tasks and who is responsible for doing what. The average household performs twenty-two hours per week of household tasks. We like to

draw a circle and make a pie chart to show the various tasks. We ask, "What would you estimate makes up the twenty-two hours of tasks in your home?" We get each person's response for each section of the pie. Frequently, family members discover how much work others are doing: "You spend four hours a week on the laundry? I had no idea!"

Next, we ask clients to assign each piece of the pie (representing time and task) to a person. This can include children and teens (and should if you have children in the home—even adult children). We call this exercise "Team Family." It is a process to affirm the work that each person does to contribute to the family. It helps family members express appreciation and gratitude to each other for the tasks they perform, and it is a way to balance the load when one or two people are doing too much. Rotate the tasks on a monthly or on a seasonal basis, but be careful about assigning certain tasks to the adult with ADD, like paying the bills or setting up an appointment with a vet. Those kinds of detailed tasks are likely to be forgotten.

4. Adapting to Challenges

Healthy families aren't perfect, but they've discovered ways—typically through trial and error—to adapt to life's challenges. Instead of throwing in the towel, blaming, or avoiding, they look for creative ways to solve any problem. Healthy families have a commitment to persevere in the face of adversity and collaborate to reach effective solutions. These are elements of resiliency. Researchers in many universities are finding that this trait is a combination of preparedness, flexibility, perseverance, and hardiness.[8] A person is more likely to be in a state of *flow*—the zone of high performance and enjoyment—if he or she has a high degree of adaptability.

Resiliency will help families with adults with ADD function at a much higher level and with a greater degree of satisfaction and happiness.

The four key behaviors of adapting to challenges (a form of resiliency) follow:

1. **Task management.** Family members effectively navigate competing activities and expectations at home, school, and work. For families with someone with ADD, we recommend using technology as much as possible to manage tasks. Google Calendar can be used to coordinate schedules. One of the best apps for personal organization is Evernote, which allows users to "capture, nurture, and share … ideas across any device," as the application tagline promises.[9] You can use Evernote to collect images and create checklists and audio files on the go. Instead of trying to track down lost sticky notes, take a photo of the note, and Evernote will store it for you. Use the reminders to pick up milk on your way home or work on the next task for your big project. If you're in a relationship, apps like this help because instead of making your spouse do it, the app can "nag" you with built-in notifications. This makes your relationship with your significant other more positive while improving your self-management skills.

2. **Adaptability.** The family adapts well when faced with changes. Each season of life offers the opportunity to grow and change—getting married, having a baby, launching a career, moving, getting promoted at work, caring for aging parents, and other opportunities require new information and skills. Adults with ADD thrive on novelty and are quickly bored and typically very adaptable.

3. **Problem solving.** Family members work together to solve problems and deal with challenges. They aren't afraid to take a risk to reach a solution. Adults with ADD can be very capable when a problem is thrust upon them. In fact, many of them thrive as emergency room doctors and nurses, paramedics, fire fighters, law enforcement officers, and professional athletes. Every day is different and requires quick decisiveness and problem solving. They enjoy the movement and challenge. Problems don't trouble them—boredom does.

4. **Democratic decision making.** Family members have a say in decisions that affect them. Adults with ADD often don't like to be told what to do, which is why so many of them become entrepreneurs. They like to have a say in the pace, style, and culture of their work. The same is true at home. Adults with ADD want to have a say in decisions involving the family—they don't have to have it their way, but they want to be heard and contribute to the discussion.

5. Connecting to Community

It really does take a village to raise a healthy family—especially a family with an adult with ADD. Family members that have relationships with neighbors and others in the community are more likely to have resilience and know where to get the help and support they need.

A family that is in touch with teachers, coaches, pastors, and counselors is more equipped to handle challenges from every facet of life. Families that are engaged in enriching activities deepen their lives and strengthen their hardiness.

A faith community like church can be a significant asset. At church, parents might develop friendships with other parents and build supportive relationships. Being the non-ADD parent can be very tiresome. Having friends from church who can help pick up your kids from soccer or take your kids to summer camp is a wonderful relief.

Adults without children can benefit from building connections with other adults through small groups, Sunday school classes, men's and women's ministries, athletic teams, retreats, and service projects. When you have an extra challenge in your life (like living with someone with ADD), it can be crucial to have friends and supportive relationships with others: "Therefore encourage one another and build each other up, just as in fact you are doing" (1 Thess. 5:11).

We all need encouragement and to be built up—especially as we seek to understand and love the adult in our life with ADD.

Treatments for ADD

In addition to cognitive behavioral therapy (CBT) as a treatment for ADD, we also suggest the following:

- education about ADD—websites, books, classes, webinars, podcasts, and so on

- emotional and social support—online groups, in-person groups, and so on
- physical exercise
- mental exercise
- school and work strategies—learn new life skills and organizational habits
- social skill strategies—an ADD coach or therapist can help with these
- thinking skills
- coaching
- self-regulation exercises—mindfulness and so on
- supplement options (more on this later)
- medication options (more on this later)
- neurofeedback strategies and brain imaging

With Nohl, we used a comprehensive treatment plan that engaged each of these approaches. He met with me weekly, in-person or via FaceTime. I assigned education so he could learn more about his ADD. I asked him to connect with the Access program at his university for emotional and social support and for accommodations for his disability. He did and was granted generous accommodations that helped him level the playing field and do well—especially in testing.

He started a daily physical exercise program of cardio and weight lifting, which could be seen in his improved posture and physique. He practiced mental exercises with an app on his phone, which reduced his anxiety and improved his concentration.

I coached him on school strategies, thinking skills, and mindfulness and encouraged him to change his diet and take supplements.

He traded his fast food for organic food and started taking supplements that enhanced brain health. I referred him to a psychiatrist who prescribed a different medication for ADD that had no side effects for Nohl. I also asked for (and received) a commitment from him to keep the pills for his own use.

Finally, I referred him to the Brain Performance Center (associated with Dr. Daniel Amen's clinics), where he received a brain scan and weekly brain training via neurofeedback.

This holistic, comprehensive approach worked for Nohl. We received clinical proof from brain scans from before treatment and six months after treatment. We observed new neuronal networks, a significant reduction of ADD activity in three different sections of Nohl's brain, and improved cognitive functioning.

Nohl's transformation serves as an example of neuroplasticity—that is, the brain's ability to grow and build new networks. We are not stuck with the brain we have; we can build a new one that functions at a higher level. Results like these give us hope that our program can be used as a treatment for ADD.

As you know, there are a variety of treatments for ADD, and most don't require a prescription. Consider the five qualities of a healthy family and reflect on how those might help your family become healthier, especially in light of the family member with ADD. Try to develop realistic expectations by using the six pointers given previously as a checklist. Finally, review the twelve possible treatments for ADD. Which would have the most benefit for the person with ADD and your family? With treatment, ADD can add color to your story—it doesn't have to define your story.

CHAPTER SIX

Living in the Common Annoyance

About five years ago, I was speaking to an attentive group of parents in San Diego. "Don't do anything for your child that he or she can do for him- or herself. Your goal is to help him or her do more as you do less. That is the key to becoming a calm and effective parent."

It was an enjoyable experience for me as a presenter. The parents laughed at my jokes, enjoyed the video clips I shared, were fully engaged at their discussion tables, asked insightful questions, and purchased a lot of books at the book table afterward. Overall, I felt pretty successful.

A few days later, I received a call from a mom. She sounded stressed and rushed. "Hi, my name is Angela, and I was at your seminar on Saturday. It was exactly what I needed. My husband says I do too much for the kids and that I need to chill. So I announced to my kids that they were going to have to step up their game. I don't want them depending on me so much. My son Derek has ADD, and I write sticky notes to remind him to do his homework, take his backpack, and do his chores. I'm always nagging him to do something, so I decided to go nag-free for a week. I told Derek I wasn't going to write a note or nag him and that I wasn't going to do anything for him that he could do for himself—including making his lunch."

"Great! I think you captured the point of my presentation," I told her.

"Oh, it's difficult to change my behavior. I've been rescuing Derek for years. I showed him where the bread and deli meat are, where the Ziploc bags and the lunch bags are, and told him that, starting on Monday, he's making his own lunch."

"How did it go?"

"I struggled with it and wanted to rescue him and make his lunch, but I resisted. But I don't know what to do now, so I'm calling you." Her voice sounded troubled.

"What happened?"

"Derek got up and made his lunch. I was so proud of him. I went about my morning, but then I got an urgent call from him at noon. He said, 'Mom, I made my lunch—just like you asked me to—but I forgot it. I left it on the counter, and I'm starved. Can you bring it to school? Please?'"

"Did you?"

"Not yet. I wasn't sure if I should, so I decided to call you. I don't want to enable him. Should I take him his lunch?"

"Well, it depends. What grade is he in?"

"He's a sophomore at San Diego State University."

I almost dropped the phone. "Seriously? A sophomore in college?"

"Yeah, why?"

"Don't take it to him. He's old enough to handle it. He won't starve, and besides, his hunger will motivate him to remember it next time."

The story is absolutely true. I can't make this stuff up. If you have an adult child who has ADD and is living at home, try not to be like this mom. She didn't prepare her son for college. She didn't empower him with tools to handle his ADD; she coddled him and made him dependent on her. Our goal is to help adult children with ADD work toward autonomy, self-reliance, and independence. If they have these traits, even developed to 60 percent, they will feel confident and capable, and they will be more likely to succeed in college, trade school, their work, and their relationships.

Have a conversation with your adult child with ADD who lives with you and ask, "How can we work together toward a common goal of you being on your own?" Write down the steps you come up with and set an appointment to continue the conversation.

What do you do if you have an adult child with ADD living at home who has mastered learned helplessness? You drop him. I learned this while in Colorado for a conference at Glen Eyrie Conference Center. I observed an eagle's nest high up on the side of a cliff. The mama eagle sat nearby to watch over her young eaglets. Every day, she would grab each youngster by the base of its neck and fly high into the sky. Once at the designated altitude, she would release her eaglet. The first day, the eaglet would plummet head over talons toward the ground. The mama eagle let him fall right past the nest.

Then she swooped down at amazing speed and grabbed the eaglet ten or fifteen feet above the rocky ground! Eventually the eaglets learned to spread their wings, and then glide a little, and then fly. One of the wilderness guides told me that if the eaglets weren't dropped, they wouldn't build the muscle, coordination, and skills to fly—they would become sitting ducks and prey to predators. What looks cruel is actually lifesaving.

Even if you succeed in teaching your child how to fly, don't make it too easy for her to remain at home—add some thorns.

The guide in Colorado also told me that after they learn to fly, the eaglets would still prefer to stay in their nest. However, the mama eagle can't hunt and provide enough food for adult eagles, so she makes the nest uncomfortable. She gathers thorns and starts packing the nest with more of them each day. Ultimately the young adult eagles think, *This nest isn't so comfortable anymore, and my siblings are really annoying. I'm going out on my own.*

Now, back to humans. What can you do to add *thorns* to your nest to make it a little less comfortable for your adult child with ADD? Are you helping her or rescuing her? Have you contributed to him developing learned helplessness? If so, announce that you will be trying a new approach—helping him do more as you do less. Not because you don't love her—but because you do.

Addicted to Drama

Adults with ADD can sometimes become addicted to creating tension. The drama makes them feel more attentive. In contrast, when they were schoolchildren, they might have been inattentive and afraid of being called on by the teacher because they weren't prepared to respond to questions. Now as adults with ADD, if a relationship, work environment, or social setting is too calm and boring, they might generate some turmoil to make it more interesting. It's a form of self-medicating.

I like what Dr. Daniel Amen wrote:

Behaviorally, many children, teens, and adults learn to get other people upset with their difficult behavior. They learn, on a purely unconscious and biological level, that when there is turmoil between people, it stimulates their brain, making them feel more alert and awake. They do not know this on a conscious level and would, in fact, deny that they ever do it. But when you watch these people with their parents or in social situations, their behavior seems goal-directed toward turmoil. After listening to hundreds of mothers, I'm convinced that this is a technique to treat underlying brain deactivation with turmoil, as an alcoholic may treat underlying restlessness or anxiety with alcohol.[1]

This was Tommy's experience. His parents divorced when he was ten. He struggled with his schoolwork. Socially, he was popular because he kept everyone entertained—except his teacher, who found his hyperactivity very annoying. Tommy would interrupt her, correct her, and refuse to respond to her discipline when he acted out. Eventually the principal suspended him for three days. His mom was working, so he could do whatever he wanted. To be at home and free to roam his neighborhood was an unintentional reward for his misbehavior. He shoplifted candy at the corner market, watched inappropriate movies on television, and stole money from his brother's room and bought a bunch of snacks.

When he went back to school, he bragged about his "vacation" to the kids on the playground. One kid threatened to tell the principal, so Tommy punched him in the mouth and said, "Try talking now, kissy!"

That got him five days at home. The principal called his mom, but she had to work and couldn't watch him. This time, Tommy's mother warned him to stay inside, but of course, he didn't—it was too boring.

He hadn't seen his dad for weeks and was mad at him for divorcing his mom. Tommy never knew the reasons. He wondered if it was his fault for being a bad kid. He wondered if his dad still loved him. Thinking about these hurtful things made him agitated. He needed something to do. He couldn't stay inside for another minute, so he went down to the park four blocks away. He climbed the fortlike play structure and sat on the roof—thirty feet above the ground. A few preschoolers and their moms were down below. Suddenly he heard some laughing and talking behind him, in the bushes on the hill. He was curious, so he climbed down and went up the hill to see who was there. A few of his brother's friends had ditched middle school and were hiding in the bushes, laughing and smoking marijuana.

They didn't like Tommy sneaking up on them, but he didn't scare off easily. He sat down with them, and eventually they offered him some weed. Tommy began his substance abuse journey at ten years old. He had brought some of his brother's money with him, so he used it to buy a few blunts from the teens. After they took off, he smoked one. The next thing he knew, a police officer was standing by him, telling him to stand up and put his hands behind his back. He was arrested for possession in fourth grade.

Tommy gave the police his dad's work number. Tommy's father came down to the station, mad as a hornet. He posted bail for juvenile court and signed the promise to appear. Tommy's dad swore at him and called him names the whole drive home, but at least he was talking to him.

Tommy continued his wild behavior through high school and through three stints of rehab as a young adult. He finally got sober after a near-death experience with a heroin overdose. Now in a federally funded Suboxone program, he was recovering from his addiction to substances, but he had a difficult time breaking his addiction to turmoil. In the span of ten days, he had accused his long-term live-in girlfriend of cheating on him, screamed obscenities at his boss at work and was fired, got into a fistfight with his brother, and was asked to leave his dad's house in the middle of a dinner for saying negative things about his dad's second wife.

Tommy was addicted to drama and refused to take any medication for his out-of-control ADD: "I want to be 100 percent drug-free," he said to me during one of our sessions.

"But you are still addicted to the chemical that is generated in your brain when you create all this drama," I replied.

Through coaching, Tommy discovered that his ADD had contributed to his substance abuse and addiction to drama. He learned skills to increase his self-awareness, becoming more alert to when he was vulnerable for an episode—namely, when he was hungry, angry, lonely, or tired (HALT)—and how to have his needs met in less dramatic ways. He stopped eating junk food. He began exercising four times a week and getting to bed before midnight. He stopped drinking coffee and energy drinks. He became calmer and less agitated. He found a job and a new girlfriend and began to patch things up with his family. He attended Narcotics Anonymous (NA) meetings three times a week and came for coaching once a week. Tommy had learned to respond instead of react. He had grown. "Now I introduce myself as Tom instead of Tommy," he said.

Shifting Gears

Brent pulled his new Porsche into the shadiest parking spot at my coaching office. He rushed inside and said, "Sorry I'm late. There was crazy traffic on PCH. I was working on a house in Malibu."

I glanced at my watch. He was ten minutes late. "No worries, we'll just have to talk fast."

"That I can do. My wife says I talk too fast. Must be a symptom of my ADD. But that's how I roll. I'm up at 5:00, work out while I listen to a podcast, shower, and hit the road by 6:20 to get to the jobsite by 7:00. As a builder, I want to make sure my contractors and subs are there on time, working, and on schedule. I race through the day, go to meetings and other jobsites, meet new clients and meet with architects, review plans, and try to get home to spend some time with my wife and kids before the kids go to bed."

Brent is a high-end builder of some of the largest and most expensive homes in Southern California—many are thirty thousand square feet and larger. His job is very demanding, but he's figured out a way to leverage his ADD: he keeps moving, uses technology, and hyperfocuses to get things done.

"My wife, Janice, asked me to bring this up with you. She really doesn't like it when I pull into the driveway and get out of my car still talking on my cell phone. I get home between 6:00 and 7:00 p.m., just in time to see the boys, play with them for a few minutes, help bathe them, get them ready for bed, and read them a quick story. The last few nights, I've been wrapping up important calls when I get home. The boys run out and grab my legs—one on the left and one on the right—and I try to walk toward the house while I'm still on the call. It's a workout with forty-plus pounds hanging on each leg! Janice stands there, hands on her hips and a frown on her face."

"I see her point. You're at work eleven or twelve hours a day, and she's home with two preschoolers. She's got the harder shift." I smiled.

"No kidding! Why do you think I work so long? I'd go crazy with those two monkeys. So what can I do? She really wants me off the phone when I get home."

"You're working in Malibu and on the west side mostly, right?"

"Yes."

"So you have a solid thirty to forty-five minutes to drive home and finish your calls?"

"If I hit traffic, it's an hour."

"Okay, here's a suggestion: Make your most important call or time-critical call first and then make the others in order of priority. When you go through the gates of your community, get off the phone. Do you shift gears in your Porsche when you slow down for the gate?"

"Yeah, I have to. The gate opens slowly, and they have a speed bump right there to make you slow down, so I downshift to second."

"That's what I want you to do—*downshift to second.* You are going through an exciting and fast-paced day in fourth and fifth gear. When you come screaming into the driveway—like it's a Formula One car pit stop—it still looks like you are in the race. Janice's day is a whole different experience with preschoolers. Enter into her world and her pace. When you downshift at the gates, get off the phone—just say, 'I'm home, I need to get off the phone'— and start praying for your wife and boys. Enter into their world. Try to imagine what kind of day they had. Ask God to help you transition, connect, listen, and have empathy. As you tune into them, you'll relax and get some distance from your frenetic day."

"So get off the phone at the gates and pray for my wife and kids?"

"Exactly."

"I can do that."

At our next session, Brent enthusiastically said, "I was off the phone when I pulled in. Janice and the boys were in our front yard, ready to welcome me home. I loved it. I felt honored. She had a huge smile, and the boys ran and shouted, 'Daddy's home!' It changed the tone of our evenings. She said I appear to be more 'present' now."

Brent and Janice needed to figure out how to navigate a busy career, parenting, and marriage with Brent's ADD. Here are some of the suggestions I shared with them:

- **See your spouse in the best light.** Assuming the best of your spouse minimizes mistrust and cynicism.

- **Be empathetic toward your spouse with ADD.** Try to see the world through his or her eyes in terms of frustrations, failures, and focus challenges.
- **Be forgiving.** Don't hold grudges or become resentful.
- **Set up regular times for talking and processing.** Doing this helps minimize resentment.
- **Keep written lists for chores and tasks.** Use technology to remind instead of nagging (see apps in the next chapter).
- **Maintain spontaneity and fun in your marriage.** Don't get in a rut.
- **Avoid designated roles.** Make sure no one is always the "designated patient" and the "caretaker."
- **Get on the same page with your parenting.** Define together what kind of people you want your children to be. Agree on how you will work together toward that goal.
- **Affirm each other.** Express gratitude and affection for each other at least five times more than you criticize.
- **Take action.** If your spouse with ADD refuses any treatment, for you to do nothing in response is "codependency"—you are protecting your spouse and preventing him or her from taking ownership of his or her ADD and growing as a person.

Kelly's Crew

I met Kelly a few years ago when she called me for help. She is a gifted artist and mother of three active boys: Cade, Colt, and Caleb. She also has ADD, as do all three of their boys—ages eleven, nine, and six. She has more of the distracted and "lost in her work" ADD, and her boys have the hyperactive kind with ridiculous amounts of energy. I've been to their house—it's barnlike, with huge windows and doors, a draft blowing through, and all kinds of weird animal noises and smells. It's relatively clean, but I could tell Kelly was more concerned about her boys having fun and her being able to focus on her sculpting and painting than having her home ready for a *Better Homes & Gardens* feature. She told me, "When my husband Craig and I moved into this house, we knew we needed to create separate spaces for my art and for the boys. We built my studio on the back of the garage, and we created a climbing wall, fort, and zip line for the kids. They love it, and most of the time, they leave me alone to work."

"Did you say zip line?" I asked.

"Yes, see the terraced slope in our yard? If you look carefully, in between the trees and all the way up is a zip line. We made it a little too high—they go too fast and don't slow down before they get to the bottom—so we added some padding for them to crash into. They will play for hours on the zip line or climbing wall. We added a parkour course this year. Their friends spend the summer over here practicing their 'PK' skills."

"For your hyperactive boys with ADD, you've made a zip line, climbing wall, and parkour course in your backyard? I've never heard of that!"

"Well, you know Craig and I are both creatives, so we knew we couldn't have a *normal* yard—not with these three guys. So we had a family meeting, asked them what they'd like to have in their backyard, and set a budget. They helped build every element. We only went a little over budget, and we finished on time. It's cheaper than a swimming pool, and they use it year-round. Plus, there's very little maintenance. Don't nominate us for parents of the year just yet; we did this as a means of survival, with three rockets going off at each other around here. We didn't want to have to pay for childcare; we wanted them to stay home but entertain themselves. If they keep busy, I can focus on my work. We did a lot of artsy things for the décor of the fort. Cade and Colt are quite gifted artists. They are both visual like me. We aren't sure about Caleb yet—he might be the most coordinated—but none of them like organized sports. They find them boring, so we built something together as a family. And we all use it. While our neighbors are struggling, putting up their 'easy-ups,' and watching four hours of boring soccer, we are home playing with our kids. It's not for everyone, but it fits us."

Kelly has discovered unique ways to keep her three active boys with ADD busy and having fun with very little supervision or direction (and no carpooling!) from her. She's also discovered the kind of workspace she needs to create and leverage her ADD to be expressive and hyperfocus on her art.

Jesse

Jesse hated family gatherings. They brought out the worst in people. His older brother picked on him and put him down. His younger brother acted needy and helpless while working on some scheme to part Mom and Dad with their money or some of their stuff. Jesse dreaded going to his parents' for Thanksgiving. Last year, he almost got into a fistfight with his older brother, Jeremy. Both have ADD and low impulse control, and both have anger issues.

Being home was stressful for Jesse. Even though he lived only a few miles away from his parents, each time he went home, it felt like going back in time to when he was a teen living with Mom and Dad. Anytime he walked into their house (which had not been remodeled since the 1980s), it was like walking into his uncomfortable past. Nothing had changed: same smell, same dingy yellow walls, and same churning in his stomach.

Jesse enjoyed talking freely among his friends about anything—sports, up-and-coming bands, celebrity gossip, tattoos, work, social media, and other interesting topics.

But his parents had a long list of forbidden topics. It made for a tense visit. And now, following their parents' dysfunctional footsteps, Jesse and Jeremy had added their own off-limits topics, but he wasn't clear what was on Jeremy's list. He never knew what would trigger his brother.

"So it's like walking on eggshells when you go home?" I asked.

"No, it's like walking on land mines. I never know where they planted a new IED. Should I just bail and go to Vegas for Thanksgiving?"

"What do you want to do?"

"Me? I'd rather go to Vegas. It's fun, and there's no drama. Actually, it's drama you pay for, not drama you feel trapped in. But holidays are a big deal for my mom. She whines about why we can't get along and just enjoy each other. She wants us to look like a greeting card on the holidays. Our family is more likely to be on a wanted poster, but for her sake, I'd like to figure out a way to get through Thanksgiving without a fight."

"Okay, realize that you have low impulse control with your ADD. That sets you and your brother up with hair triggers for anger. Plus you have a valid reason for reacting—he tormented you growing up, and he still puts you down. There are three things you can do. First, bring your healthiest adult self to the holiday. Work out, get enough sleep, practice the mindfulness skills I showed you, and avoid sugar, alcohol, and drugs, except your prescription for ADD."

"Sounds like detox."

"Exactly. You want to go in sober, calm, and nonreactive. Your family is toxic enough."

He smiled. "Yeah, that would definitely help. I notice I'm in a better mood after I work out and avoid junk food and sugar. I don't drink anymore, and that's really helped stabilize my mood."

"I'm guessing when you and Jeremy went off on each other, both of you had been drinking?"

"Yes, and he was on something else too."

"Second, realize that you are an adult, not a child. So bring the healthiest *adult* to the holiday. Not a teen, not an angry college student, and not a resentful son. Just be neutral. You don't have to pretend you are walking into the perfect television family, and you don't have to rehearse decades of hurt. Start that day with a clean slate—one day at a time."

"Yeah, I learned that phrase at a meeting. What's the third step?" Jesse asked as he quickly typed notes into his phone.

"Be aware that the physical act of walking into your family home might trigger you and cause you to regress—go back to when you were a rebellious teen and lived with a mean brother and dysfunctional parents. You might regress to your old role, and they might regress to their former roles as well. It's the same house, he's the same brother, but you are now an adult who has matured, is healthier, has more self-control and more self-awareness, and can set boundaries."

"I think I can do that. I'll need some help setting those boundaries."

"I can help you with that next session, but here's a tip that will help in the meantime: don't stay as long. Instead of hanging out there all day, tell your mom you'll need to leave by a certain time because you and your girlfriend have plans. Make some plans so you aren't lying, but they can be anything. I'd suggest something that your brother would never do."

"What's that?"

"You and your girlfriend serve Thanksgiving dinner to the homeless at the rescue mission."

"Perfect! Nailed it!" He smiled and extended his fist for a bump.

You might be able to relate to Jesse's situation of walking on land mines when he gets together with his family. Or maybe you are like Angela, a parent who has done too much for her adult child and finds that he has learned helplessness. Or maybe your ADD reminds you of Tommy's experience of being addicted to substances and drama.

Take a moment to reflect on these situations. Which one can you best relate to?

If you are married and either you or your spouse have ADD, which of the tips for living with a spouse with ADD would you like to work on first?

Kelly and Craig chose to embrace, understand, and love their three hyper, physical, noisy sons. There are ways to live with ADD and make it fun. A zip line might not work for your family, but what would?

CHAPTER SEVEN

Best Intentions Paving Company

Comedian Jeff Foxworthy has a well-known routine called "You might be a redneck if …"[1] For instance, "You might be a redneck if … you cut your grass and found a car." In his routine, he offers hilarious commentary on the blue-collar, redneck lifestyle.

We thought an adaptation of his routine might be fun. So here is "You might be a person with ADD if":

- You go to buy groceries at the store, but you forget the list and the one very important thing you went there for in the first place.
- You bring the groceries in from the car and place them on the kitchen counter, but you get distracted by what's on television and forget to put them away.
- You're considered the "life of the party," but you're always late to the party because you lost two things: track of time and your car keys.
- You don't like to be criticized for your "disorganization" just because you have six piles of random papers on your desk. There's a method to your organizational madness—if only you could remember what it is.

the connection first. We ask parents to memorize this: "First connect, then direct."

2. **Think long-range.** Who do you want your child to be physically, mentally, emotionally, socially, and spiritually when he or she becomes an adult? We often use Christ's example as a best practice for how we want our kids to turn out: "And Jesus grew in wisdom and stature and in favor with God and man" (Luke 2:52).

   Jesus grew in *wisdom*, which is knowledge applied to life. It's more than excelling at academics. He grew in *stature*, which means he grew physically. He also grew in *favor with God*, meaning He grew spiritually, and He grew socially, or *in favor with man*.

   Try an exercise that we call "Target 18." Make a list of qualities that you want your child to reflect by the time they reach eighteen years of age. These can be character traits, skills, and other virtues.

   Record these as *attributes*. Then think through specific *behaviors* for each attribute.

   For example, if you have "integrity" as one of your attributes, corresponding behaviors could be "tells the truth" or "is trustworthy."

   Finally, determine a consequence for each attribute and behavior. Decide on a positive consequence and a negative consequence. If your child is ten years old or older, involve them in setting the consequences. We call this the "ABCs for Effective Parenting." In chart form, it looks like this:

Attribute	Behavior	Consequences
Integrity	• Tells the truth • Is trustworthy • Doesn't hide the truth	**+ Positive** Gets to stay overnight with friends
		– Negative No overnights

This strategy reduces the drama, escalation, and threats that often occur with parents and children with ADD. Parents can remain calm and refer to the chart, which is written and posted somewhere. (Keep backups—they tend to disappear.) If you have a conflict, you can follow this script:

> "I see by your behavior that you aren't showing integrity. You aren't telling the truth. What is your consequence?"
>
> The child responds, "I dunno."
>
> "Yes, you do. You signed the ABC chart. When you lie, you lose the privilege of spending Friday night at your friends. That's your consequence." (Hint to parent: immediately walk away to avoid the backlash.)

3. **Don't escalate when disciplining.** You can see how the ABCs allow you to stay focused and deal with misbehavior and discipline but not get into a fight about it. We encourage parents to stay calm and recite the mantra, "It's your decision. You knew the consequences."

ADD children will often get a buzz—an adrenaline rush—when they argue with a parent. Don't reward them with the thrill. Children with ADD are disappointed by a calm and firm response, but it's very effective.[2]

The goal of discipline is to teach, not punish. Yelling, screaming, and nagging can be destructive and are ineffective and often addictive for the ADD child.

Mean what you say. Say what you mean. Be consistent.

4. **Spend one-on-one time with your child each day.** Even fifteen minutes focused on your child with ADD will enhance his or her self-esteem and sense of value and likely minimize acting out to get your attention. Develop a daily routine if you can (e.g., play with Legos, walk the dog, read, play a game, kick a ball—do whatever your child considers fun).

5. **Notice and affirm positive behavior.** Children with ADD receive many critical comments. Look for ways to affirm your child. Aim for at least seven affirmations for each criticism or correction. Your affirmation will help your child notice and affirm what they like about themselves instead of allowing their ADD to shape a critical self-image.

When Your Parent Has ADD

Much of what's been written about ADD has been about children and teens, but what can you do if your parent is exhibiting ADD behavior? If your relationship with your parent is strong and safe, you could mention something like, "Mom, you know that my wife and I have recently had our son diagnosed with ADD as an adult, and he's getting treatment. Honestly, I think I might see some similar symptoms at times with you. What do you think? How do you manage to stay focused?"

By asking the two-pronged question, you are giving her an out. She can choose to respond to the second question with "Yes, I get distracted, but I've learned to …" or she might respond to the first. In either case, you've started a conversation. If she agrees to get help, the following section describes what it could look like.

For most adults, effective treatment of ADD involves the following:

1. **Diagnosis.** Effective treatment begins with an accurate diagnosis. Many adults have told us that they felt relieved after they received their diagnosis of ADD: "Finally, an explanation for the different way my brain works!"

2. **Education.** The more you know about ADD, the more likely you are to develop a treatment plan that works for your unique type of ADD and your personality.

3. **Structuring.** Executive functioning is typically low for people with ADD. As a result, adults with ADD need strong external structures to compensate: accountability, visual prompts and reminders, appointment books, timers, goals, daily and weekly agendas, budgets, and lists are crucial to keep the adult with ADD focused and on-task. Thankfully, we now have a host of apps we can utilize for structure right on our phones.

4. **Coaching and/or psychotherapy.** An ADD coach or life coach is someone who is trained to offer encouragement,

direction, accountability, and process for the adult with ADD. An effective coach will help the client move from impulsively reacting to intentionally responding. Adults with ADD thrive with structured and positive coaching. Coaching encourages the development of insight, which is one of the most transformative skills for adults with ADD. Some therapists are adding the coaching element to their practice so they can be more directive with ADD clients. Coaches might also recommend traditional psychotherapy if the ADD adult is also experiencing depression, high anxiety, or other diagnoses.

5. **Medication or alternatives.** Some adults with ADD are opposed to taking medication. We've found that this opinion has often been shaped by anecdotal experiences or old data rather than up-to-date scientific evidence. People will say things like "I don't want to change my personality; if I take meds, I'll become a zombie." There are so many newer medications that work very well for adults with ADD, and many not only improve focus but also address the angst and anxiety that are common with adult ADD. The medication corrects a chemical imbalance of neurotransmitters in the parts of the brain that control impulses and regulate attention, focus, and mood. Medication by itself is not the answer, but the right prescription can provide significant relief, and if used properly, it is very safe. About 85 percent of adults will benefit from one of the several medications now available for ADD.[3] For adults who still won't consider medication, we suggest alternatives (see chapter eight).

When Your Teen Has ADD

Fourteen-year-old Ryan tapped his right foot up and down. At any given time, some body part moved. His teachers had labeled him "hyper and distracted," and every year, they recorded *incidents* in his permanent record. His parents were desperate to have him do better at his private high school. His older sister was an excellent student there and was now at an elite college as a freshman.

"I don't like having the same last name as my sister. Everyone expects me to be like her, and I'm not. Never have been. Never will be," Ryan said. He looked down at his shoes and realized he was tapping. He stopped his foot, but almost immediately, his right hand drummed on the arm of the chair in my office.

"What are you good at?" I asked.

He looked somewhat shocked. "I've been to lots of shrinks, and nobody has asked me that. They always focus on my problem, my grades, or my diagnosis. Hmm … let me think. Oh, I know, I'm good at video games. I dominate at *Grand Theft Auto*."

"Where else do you dominate?"

He smiled at my use of his word. "I'm good at volleyball. Obviously, I'm tall and can block and spike. But unless I raise my grades, I'll be academically ineligible, and that sucks because I'm the second-best player on the team. The best player is a kid named Colin, and he's likely to be moved up to varsity—as a freshman! How amazing is that? Coach said I could be too if I had better grades. Varsity needs a middle blocker like me."

I had noticed Ryan's height when he came in—all six feet and two inches. His mom said that he was on a growth spurt and that she couldn't keep him in shoes or pants, so he wore shorts year-round. "So you have a passion for volleyball and video games. What else?" I asked.

"I'm addicted to my phone. I'm always on it—connecting with friends and sharing videos, funny memes, and photos that we edit with crazy special effects. It's the usual teenage waste of time, according to my parents. Is that a skill?"

"It can be. Or it can be a huge time-suck."

"I know. I'm a lot like that dog in the animated movie that sees a squirrel and gets distracted. I'm very intrigued by any visual distraction, plus I can't sit still."

"I thought you might say that. Let's finish by walking around the grounds. It's like a park outside—with trees, waterfalls, fish, bridges, and a gazebo."

"Perfect! I'm sick of being inside. Our school is all indoors. We don't get to go outside between classes. I get so cooped up. I prefer to be outside."

As we walked outside, Ryan appeared more at ease. Movement used up his excess energy. "I've never done this with a shrink. This is cool. I'm sorry—are you offended by that term?"

"Technically, I'm not a shrink. But no, I'm not offended. I'm a coach, so I'm more like your volleyball coach, who might tell you what you are doing well and how you can improve."

"That, I can relate to." He paused to watch the carp swimming by the waterfall. "I could reach in and grab that big orange one right now!"

"Yeah, you could," I agreed.

He smiled and started walking again. "So how do I raise my grades so I can play on the team?"

"Do you ever forget assignments?"

"Yes."

"Do you complete homework but forget to turn it in?"

"All the time."

"Do you have to work on a project with a group?"

"Yes, this semester."

"Are you more likely to look at an assignment notebook or an app on your phone?"

"App on my phone. Definitely."

"Okay, I have the sweet suite of apps for you to use to help you with all that."

"The school provides an online system, but my parents can't figure it out, and it's typically three days behind."

"Would you like to see a graphic illustration of your progress on your homework or a group project?"

"Yeah, that would be cool. I'd rather get the props versus focusing on the work left."

"Okay, then you can use Trello[4] as a visual way to give yourself props and for those in your group project to see what you've done. We can download it when we get back to my office. It's free. Do you use Google Docs and Google Calendar?"

He pulled out his phone. "Got 'em both right here, on my tablet, and on my laptop."

"Perfect! You can easily sync those with Trello and Evernote. Evernote is cool because you can work on projects on various devices, and it syncs with them and is searchable.[5] Let's say your teacher puts up a diagram on the board. Get permission to use your phone—she knows you have accommodations for your ADD—and take a picture of it. Tag it with something you will remember and save it in Evernote. You can search for photos, documents, notes, receipts, media, and just about anything else, so you won't lose stuff. You can create in Google Docs, save to Evernote, and sync with Trello, and you can set reminders with Google Calendar. The piece of accurate data you need is a list of projects, tests, and due dates for two weeks at a time. You add those to your calendar, set up your reminders, and follow them."[6]

"Sounds cool and easy—an excuse to play around with apps on my phone."

"But you still have to do the work. What you need are two motivators, maybe three."

"Well, one motivator is that if I raise my grades, I get to play volleyball."

"Write that down in your notes on your phone right now under 'Motivators.'"

We stopped walking, and within ten seconds, Ryan said, "Done."

"What else motivates you?"

"Not looking like I'm the stupid kid because I have ADD."

"Yeah, being proud of your grades and getting props for them."

"Absolutely. I'll never be the nerd my sister is, but I'm an athlete and she's not."

"Write that down as motivator two: 'Proud of myself.'"

He wrote it down. "You said three?"

"Instead of your parents nagging, how about if you show them how you are using all these integrated apps to stay on top of your stuff. Try doing this four nights a week for five minutes. Either you take the initiative or they hunt you down and nag you. What do you think?"

"Deal. I'm gonna write 'Show, don't nag.'"

"If you do that for eight nights—Monday through Thursday for two school weeks, what would you like as a reward from your parents?"

"Besides the time they aren't yelling at me?" He grinned sarcastically.

"Yeah."

"I'd like the new Madden football video game."

"Good idea. I'll pitch it to your parents."

Ryan reached out, and we bumped fists.

Two weeks later, Ryan had maximized his integrated digital personal organizational strategy, raised his grades, and earned the video game.

When Your Spouse Has ADD

When we work with couples where one (or both) have ADD, we like to use a lot of visual tools. People with ADD tend to be more visual. One of the tools we use is the "ADD Dance." We draw a circle with arrows pointing clockwise around it to indicate movement. We like to explain it like this:

"When you have a partner with ADD, it can add a lot of flavor to your relationship, but you need to know what form of dance you are doing. With a partner with ADD, you aren't doing the waltz—you are more likely to be doing a mash-up of salsa and hip-hop. The

ADD Dance provides lots of flavor and some freestyle added in. Notice the top of the circle says *Harmony*. You are dancing together in rhythm and enjoying each other's company. Let's add a happy face here. But then your ADD partner gets distracted. Notice the next word to the right on the circle is *Distraction*. It could be any symptom of ADD, but for dancing, distraction has the most negative impact. Let's write *squirrel* here. Other symptoms could be forgetfulness, disorganization, not listening, and so on. The reaction to that symptom is next—note the next arrow and the words *Hurt/React*. I'm going to add *steps on toes* because if you aren't paying attention, you will lose focus and step on your partner's toes. This will create pain in her life. She will react, and you will have lost your harmony. The next action in the ADD Dance is *Withdraw*. One or both of you will pull away from the other to protect your toes. So instead of harmony, closeness, rhythm, and happiness, you have danced your way into disharmony, withdrawal, distance, and a lack of rhythm. Someone is mad, which is the next arrow and action: *Anger*. When someone gets mad in a relationship where one of the adults has ADD, it usually exacerbates their symptoms of ADD. Note the next arrow and the words *Symptoms Increase*. I'm going to add a sad face, because at this point in the dance, one or both of you don't want to dance anymore. It's no longer fun."

We use this analogy to show systemic patterns in couples where one or both have ADD. Most couples laugh when they see the ADD Dance illustrated and add, "That's exactly what we do!" But their admission represents a lot of smashed toes. It represents a lot of pain.

When your spouse has ADD, the first step is to become aware of how you do this dance as a couple. Observe how you trigger each other. Notice how you each contribute to the escalation of drama. We like to erase the whiteboard and write three words: *observe*, *own*, and *options*.

Observe how you do the dance. Then own your part (rather than casting blame). Finally, discuss what you could do differently—those are your options. Here are some options for couples with ADD:

- Keep a sense of humor; keep dancing.
- Learn as much as you can about ADD.
- Have a daily check-in time to talk about your day. Each person can talk about anything he or she wants for three minutes.
- Choose one way to add a reminder for the person with ADD to remember a task (use your phone, sticky notes, whiteboard, note in car, etc.).
- Celebrate the small wins and even the failures, because now the odds are in your favor.
- Avoid the stereotypical roles of child/parent, broken/healer, victim/rescuer, or mess-maker/cleaner-upper.
- Don't use your ADD as an excuse; learn how to leverage it to harness its power for good.

When Your Coworker Has ADD

If your coworker has told you that she has ADD, you might have noticed that she thinks differently than other people. This can be a huge asset in most work environments. Thinking outside of the box, taking calculated risks, responding well in crises, and surpassing the status quo are all qualities that can produce a driven, positive change agent at work.

But there might come a time when she asks for your help or you notice that symptoms of ADD are having a negative impact on her work or on the team. What do you do?

First of all, ask for her permission: "Do I have your permission to make some suggestions that I think will help benefit our productivity?"

If she agrees, affirm two or three strengths that she has that add value to the company.

Then say, "In addition to those strengths, I have some ideas that could help us go to the next level. Are you open to hearing those? It will take just a few minutes."

If she agrees, go ahead and share. She might choose to schedule it for later.

When she has the time, repeat what you said earlier about her strengths, perhaps paraphrasing a little so you don't sound redundant.

There might come a time when she asks for your help or you notice that symptoms of ADD are having a negative impact on her work or on the team. What do you do?

Here is an imaginary scenario illustrating how you might help your co-worker with ADD:

"Remember when you told me that you have ADD?"

"Yes, that was at lunch at Cucina Verona."

"In addition to your strengths, I've seen a few evidences of ADD that you might not be aware of. I'd like to call your attention to them, and you can decide if my input is valid and if you want to address it. I think it will benefit our productivity as a team and yours individually. By the way, this is just between you and me."

"Okay, go ahead."

"I'm not the expert on this, but it seems like we get stuck when things aren't clear. I think it would benefit the team if we could enhance clarity and capture what is most important and then stick to it. I've noticed that if things aren't clear, we lose momentum because we don't have alignment. When you come up with an issue, we aren't sure if it is a priority or just your latest idea."

"Okay, but I'm just a member of the team—I'm not the boss."

"But you are our best innovator. We need that. So I have some suggestions for how we can have your input without it sidetracking us."

"What are they?"

"When you have a new idea, run it by me first instead of the entire team. I'll help you review it in light of our workload and our priorities, and then we can decide how to refine it and present it to the team. I think we should capture it on paper, let it marinate, then evaluate."

"Marinate, then evaluate. I like that."

"It's not entirely original with me. I read *Getting Things Done* by David Allen, and he suggests five steps: (1) capture the idea, (2) clarify the concept, (3) organize it, (4) reflect, and finally, (5) engage and do.[7] I added the marinate part because I like to cook."

"That book sounds interesting."

"I thought you'd be interested. Maybe you noticed how organized my workspace is now? I found that things that were piled
and didn't have a place were adding stress and distracting me."

"Oh, I see where this is going. My workspace is a mess!"

"I memorized something from the book that helped me: 'Anything that does not belong where it is, the way it is, is an *open loop*
pulling on your attention.' I have a copy at my desk. Do you want
to read it and discuss it together at lunch?"[8]

"Yes, that sounds like something I could use. I have lots of open
loops." She smiled. "Thanks."

People with ADD have the best intentions, but they can become
distracted or lose focus and not follow through. In this chapter,
we've offered lots of tips for how to understand and relate to someone with ADD—a child, a parent, a teen, a spouse, or a coworker.
If you are the person with ADD, you might recognize yourself
in the examples. You might find yourself doing the ADD Dance
with your husband or wife. What one suggestion seems to be the
most relevant to you? What small habit would produce the biggest
positive impact? Are you willing to try implementing it this week?

CHAPTER EIGHT

Going the Distance

The predawn sky morphed from indigo to pale gray over the Pacific. Dawn patrol—6:17 a.m., Ventura, California. We sipped coffee, hoping it would warm us up before we pulled off our hoodies, donned our wetsuits, and geared up for the brain-freeze chill of the winter swell. "What's the water temperature, Kyle?"

"It was fifty-four when I went yesterday. Not too nippy," he answered. Kyle could go surfing any day he wanted. He was self-employed and scheduled his work around the surf. He was in terrific shape for a guy over fifty; he could out-surf most guys half his age. Of course, his devotion to the waves might explain why his marriage fell apart. But the single life seemed to suit him and his ADD. Kyle would say, "I don't like commitments. I just want to ebb and flow."

His life was textbook ADD—lots of starts and stops. At one time, he had a huge business with lots of employees, but he had some conflict with his foreman, so the foreman quit and took half of the crew to start his own company. It turned out that most of his crew was fed up with his impulsiveness, his forgetting to do payroll on time, and his demands that they finish more jobs in fewer days.

He sold what was left of that company, bought a boat, and moved to the South Pacific, where he could surf and charter his boat for fishing and surf trips. It didn't work out, and he moved back to California. He was depressed, angry, embarrassed, and blamed everyone, especially his wife. She got fed up and divorced him. He started up his business again, but this time he did all the work—no employees. All he had to manage was himself, and that was a challenge.

I could tell Kyle was in a dark mood as he pulled the Toyota Tacoma off the 101 and into the dirt parking lot of Emma Wood State Beach.

"I don't know, man," he said. "Business is good, I have enough money, the surf has been good—look at it." He pointed through the windshield toward the eight-foot peaks. "But I feel stuck. I've messed up my businesses, my marriage, and I'm not sure why I'm still here on the planet."

My first thought was that Kyle had gone back to drinking. He got sober after his divorce. His ex recently told me, "He's nicer sober, but that ship's sailed."

I asked him, "Are you still going to meetings?"

"Oh, yeah! Almost two years sober this month. I'm not that desperate or foolish. I'm an idiot when I drink. I have no control over my mouth or my behavior."

We got out of the truck and put on our wetsuits. "How do you feel stuck?" I asked.

"Spinning my wheels. Lacking some goal or purpose. I can't stay focused. I get easily knocked off my game. Right now, I feel overwhelmed, and don't know where to start." He sat on his tailgate and slipped on his booties.

So this was going to be a surf therapy session, I noted to myself. "I coach people who feel overwhelmed and stuck. I offer them evidenced-based solutions. Want to hear what I tell them?"

"Do I have to pay you for it?"

"No, just buy a breakfast burrito afterward."

"Deal."

"Healthy people have setbacks, but they keep moving forward. They might get overwhelmed, but they follow the three Cs of resilience. Resilience is hardiness to persevere and bounce back from defeat. It has an element of flex to it. The first *C* stands for control—you tell yourself, 'I can always do something,' and you think of some small action you can take to get out of the passive victim mode."

"Yeah, that mode is risky, especially for an addict. What's the second?"

I pulled my board out of my board bag. "Commitment. You take a few minutes and ask, 'What's important to me? What are my values?' When we get sidetracked or overwhelmed, we lose our sense of self. By asking what's important to us, we rediscover who we are. It adds clarity."

"I like that word, *clarity*. Most of my thinking is fuzzy. That's when I make my worst decisions—fuzzy, impulsive decisions."

"No doubt. That's typical of ADD running your life. But these can help you focus. The third *C* stands for challenge. You look at a challenge in your life and write it down. You look at it like it's an opponent in an upcoming game. Then you come up with a game plan to contend with that particular opponent."

"Oh, I like that. It's like applying sports to life. Each game is different because each opponent is unique."

"Exactly. Make sure your game plan is strategic and dynamic. Plan an 'if-then' scenario. Let me show you how to apply all three Cs of resiliency. Let's say I'm feeling a lack of purpose. I tell myself, 'I can always do something.' Then I think of one small thing to do. For me, I think better after surfing. It relaxes me and clears my mind."

"Me too." He smiled and nodded at the set.

"So to take control, we go surfing. Then we ask, 'What is important? What am I committed to?' What would you say is important to you?"

Kyle looked at a seagull flying overhead. "Ahh … I suppose I would have to say it's important for me to stay sober, because I want a future, I want a wife, I want a family."

"And you can be committed to working toward those values?"

"Yes—definitely."

"So what's the challenge? What's your game plan with an 'if-then' strategy?"

"*If* I want to have a future, *then* I better focus on making my business more profitable. I need to bill people quicker and not wait. And for a girlfriend or wife, *if* I want to meet the right woman, *then* I need to look for her in the right places. My friends tell me to sign up for eHarmony, but I keep forgetting."

"So there's your game plan for more money and better odds of meeting a compatible match. Now you implement the strategy and tell someone when you will finish the game—a deadline."

"I'll do those two things by next Friday when we surf. I'll bill all my clients from the last six weeks, and I'll sign up for eHarmony. I like it—skills, not pills."

"And one more thing?"

Kyle didn't turn his head but focused on a surfer dropping into an overhead barrel. "What's that?"

"You'll buy me a breakfast burrito, remember?"

A Common Myth

Kyle is like so many of our friends and clients—he has significant ADD but is not willing to try medication. Kyle tried a prescription from his medical doctor ten years ago, but it left him with side effects, so he quit taking it after six months. With his sobriety, he didn't want to risk abusing anything, so he wanted to find alternatives.

Before we talk about alternatives, we'd like to challenge the myth that if you take medication for ADD, you are more likely to abuse substances. Consider what Dr. Daniel Amen—a psychiatrist and expert on ADD—wrote: "A very common myth in the lay community is that the use of medication to treat ADD children somehow predisposes them to drug abuse in later life. The theory is that giving children or teens medicine to help their ADD somehow teaches them to abuse substances later on. Both my clinical experience and research shows that, in fact, the opposite is true. Treating ADD decreases drug or alcohol abuse later on."[1]

My clinical experience supports Dr. Amen's claim. I've observed that properly prescribed ADD medications reduce the likelihood of substance abuse.

A few years ago, I had a huge influx of teen clients with addictions. The teens had all been busted for using and often selling drugs. Some were as young as thirteen. We got the teens started on the road to recovery, but I noticed that the parents were underserved. I talked with one of the moms, who ironically happened to also work as a registered nurse in residential treatment for addictions. She said, "There are services and support for the teens, but nothing for the parents."

Since the kids were *partying*, we decided the parents needed a party. The nurse and I launched PARTY—Parents of At-Risk & Troubled Youth—a support group open to parents in the community. We were shocked at how many parents contacted us to join. Youth pastors, school counselors, and therapists referred parents. We had to cap it at twenty-four members, with twenty-seven on a waiting list for the next session in the spring.

The second week, my colleague (the nurse) shared, "We took my son, Tyson, to be diagnosed for ADD. The psychiatrist said that a lot of kids with ADD self-medicate with marijuana and opiates. My husband and I had no idea, and I'm a nurse. Tyson's risk-taking and low impulse control are factors found in addicts. I have business cards from the psychiatrist. I'll pass them around."

We met for thirteen weeks. Each week, a parent or two reported the same thing: his or her child had ADD. At the end of our time, different doctors, psychiatrists, psychologists, and therapists diagnosed all twenty-four teens with ADD. There is definitely a correlation between untreated ADD and substance abuse. Some current researchers are reporting that it's causational, not simply correlative.

Why bring up the teen stories if this is a book about adult ADD? Because adults with ADD have had it since they were children and teens. The majority of adults don't outgrow the symptoms, but they often find ways to minimize them and leverage them as strengths. But if adults are in denial about their ADD or not aware of the negative side effects, they are at risk for substance abuse.

Alternatives to Medications[2]

Whether you take medication for your ADD or not, start with a 100 percent multivitamin and mineral supplement. It's difficult with our life-in-the-fast-lane families to plan nutritious, well-balanced meals to eat at home, and it's especially hard for families in which one or more people have ADD. They are more likely to swing through the drive-through; hence the need for the vitamins and minerals.

Another group of helpful supplements to take (whether you take medication or not) are omega-3 fatty acids. Children and adults with ADD have been found to have low levels of omega-3 fatty acids in their bloodstream. We need omega-3s to feed our brain two major components: docosahexaenoic acid (DHA) and eicosapentaenoic acid (EPA). EPA is more stimulating, while DHA tends to be sedating. Adults should take 2,000 to 4,000 milligrams daily.

Omega-3 fatty acids can be found in oily fish, nuts, olive oil, and flaxseed. These nutrients help with memory and general cognitive function. The best source of omega-3s is fish oil. But if you are like us, you don't like the taste of fish oil, and even the tablets or capsules can taste too fishy. We like the "nutrition that tastes like dessert" that we found in the smoothie-like Barlean's Omega Swirl (www.barleans.com/swirls). It's the tastiest way to get the benefits of fish oil without any fishy taste, and it has the recommended daily allotment of vitamin D, which is essential for optimal brain function. (Our favorite flavors are Mango Peach, Citrus Sorbet, and Lemon Zest.)

ADDitude Magazine editors did a comprehensive review of dozens of studies that indicate that omega-3s are about 40 percent as effective as stimulant medications in treating ADD symptoms. And of course, there are no side effects, unless you can't stand smoothies.[3]

The brain is 60 percent fat by dry weight. Most of that fat is DHA, a long chain omega-3 fatty acid. DHA deficiency can accentuate the symptoms of ADD and depression. Omega-3 DHA has a calming and anti-inflammatory effect.

There are many other supplements that are popular for treating ADD, but they act differently with the seven different types of ADD, so we won't address them here. Again, discuss with your doctor before adding supplements to medications.

Brain Foods

Eat brain-healthy foods to maximize brain performance and minimize ADD symptoms. Most professionals who treat ADD suggest a diet with each meal full of fruits and vegetables, complex carbohydrates, and a serving of lean protein. Food can be used as brain medicine.

Many of us start the day with coffee, pancakes, cereal, toast, or donuts. These are high in simple carbs and are terrible for concentration and focus. Your body quickly converts the carbs to sugar, giving you a quick spike in blood sugar, and then drops you with an insulin release that makes you feel foggy, tired, spacey, and inattentive, so you need another cup of coffee—and it's only 9:24 a.m.

Start the day out right and feed your brain. Try a brain-healthy breakfast of hard-boiled eggs, nuts, chopped fresh veggies, and fresh fruit. Only have juice if it's organic and without preservatives and sugar.

For lunch, skip the fast-food burgers, pasta, bread, and french fries and try grilled fish, a salmon salad, or a piece of meat with grilled veggies. Skip the simple carbohydrates at lunch and notice how alert you feel and how much more energy you have. No need to take a siesta!

When you get hungry and need a snack, eat a few raw almonds and a piece of fresh fruit (apples, berries), and you will get an increase in the neurotransmitter dopamine, which is involved in motivation, focus, emotional significance, relevance, and pleasure. Avocados and lima beans work too. Guacamole, anyone?

Faith Matters

Whether you look at ADD as a weakness or strength or somewhere in between, having ADD means your brain works differently. That doesn't mean you are weird or less valuable or broken; it just means that you experience life differently, and you learn differently than people without ADD. God didn't wring His hands when He crafted you, exclaiming, "Oops! I made another one with ADD!" He made you this way according to His design. You aren't a mistake—you are a masterpiece: "I praise you because I am fearfully and wonderfully made; your works are wonderful, I know that full well. My frame was not hidden from you when I was made in the secret place, when I was woven together in the depths of the earth. Your eyes saw my unformed body; all the days ordained for me were written in your book before one of them came to be. How precious to me are your thoughts, God!" (Ps. 139:14–17).

Having this long-range point of view gives meaning and design to ADD; a short-range focus tends to be more self-centered and reactive. People with ADD tend to live in the moment and make decisions based on their feelings (which may change hourly). A long-range view can add stability and consistency and mitigate reactivity.

We need someone like you to complete our village. People with ADD play a critical role in the community, including the community of faith: "All these are empowered by one and the same Spirit, who apportions to each one individually as he wills. For just as the body is one and has many members, and all the members of the body, though many, are one body, so it is with Christ … God arranged the members in the body, each one of them as he chose" (1 Cor. 12:11, 12, 18 ESV).

If someone in your life has ADD, extend grace to him or her every day. It will force you to stretch and grow. Interacting with someone with ADD will test your patience. When you reach the end of your natural human patience, tap into the superpower from the Holy Spirit, which you have within you as a follower of Christ: "But the fruit of the Spirit is love, joy, peace, *patience*, kindness, goodness, faithfulness" (Gal. 5:22 ESV, emphasis added).

At times, you might feel like ADD gets in your way, or if you have someone with ADD in your life, you might become annoyed by his or her symptoms. Let's face it—ADD can be intrusive. When it becomes intrusive, it seems less like *creative genius* and more like a bothersome liability. You aren't alone—even Paul felt this way: "But he said to me, 'My grace is sufficient for you, for my power is made perfect in weakness.' Therefore I will boast all the more gladly of my weaknesses, so that the power of Christ may rest upon me" (2 Cor. 12:9 ESV).

God doesn't need superstar, flawless, perfect people. He chooses average humans to demonstrate His power. When we allow Him to show up in our weakness, and when we are okay with meeting Him in the center of our weakness, He begins a process of redemption for His purposes. We don't fully understand it from our limited human brains, but we know one thing: God's power working in our weakness is His grace at work.

And sometimes, that's all we need—grace—whether we are trying to understand and love someone with ADD or trying to understand and love our ADD selves.

Notes

Introduction

1   For clarity, we prefer the older term ADD—attention deficit disorder. ADD, with the listed subtypes, can be more specific and accurate than ADHD—attention deficit hyperactivity disorder. Not all people with ADD have hyperactivity, so the *H* isn't necessary in some diagnoses. Our preference is reflected in our choice to use ADD instead of ADHD in this book.

Chapter One

1   National Institute of Mental Health (NIMH), "Attention Deficit Hyperactivity Disorder," last updated March 2016, www.nimh.nih.gov/health/topics/attention-deficit -hyperactivity-disorder-adhd/index.shtml.

2   Daniel G. Amen, *Healing ADD: The Breakthrough Program That Allows You to See and Heal the 7 Types of ADD* (New York: Berkley Books, 2013), xxvii.

3   Alan Schwartz and Sarah Cohen, "A.D.H.D. Seen in 11% of U.S. Children as Diagnoses Rise," *New York Times,* March 31, 2013, www.nytimes.com/2013/04/01health/ morediagnoses-of-hyperactivity-causing-concern.

4   NIMH, "Attention Deficit Hyperactivity Disorder."

5   American Academy of Pediatrics, "Children in Foster Care Three Times More Likely to Have ADHD Diagnosis," October 23, 2015, www.aap.org/en-us/about-the-aap/aap

-press-room/pages/Children-in-Foster-Care-Three-Times
-More-Likely-to-Have-ADHD-Diagnosis.aspx.

6   NIMH, "Attention Deficit Hyperactivity Disorder."

7   Amen, *Healing ADD,* xxxv.

8   Amen, *Healing ADD,* xxxiv–xxxv.

9   Melissa Orlov, *The ADHD Effect on Marriage: Understand and Rebuild Your Relationship in Six Steps* (Plantation, FL: ADD Warehouse, 2010), 5.

Chapter Two

1   Dale Archer, *The ADHD Advantage: What You Thought Was a Diagnosis May Be Your Greatest Strength* (New York: Penguin Random House, 2015), 20.

2   Edward M. Hallowell and John J. Ratey, *Driven to Distraction: Recognizing and Coping with Attention Deficit Disorder from Childhood through Adulthood* (New York: Anchor Books, 2011), 87, adapted.

3   Hallowell and Ratey, *Driven to Distraction,* 335, adapted.

Chapter Three

1   Dale Archer, *The ADHD Advantage: What You Thought Was a Diagnosis May Be Your Greatest Strength* (New York: Penguin Random House, 2015), 63, emphasis added.

2   Archer, *ADHD Advantage,* 82, adapted.

3   Judy Dutton, "ADHD Athletes: Inspiring Sports Stars with Attention Deficit," *ADDitude,* June/July 2006.

4   Keath Low, "Adam Levine Talks about ADHD," *Verywell,* last updated February 14, 2017, www.verywell.com/adam -levine-talks-about-adhd-20602, adapted.

5   Zooey Deschanel, *HelloGiggles* (blog), hellogiggles.com/ author/zooey-deschanel/.

6   "Can't Stop the (ADHD) Feeling!," *ADDitude,* accessed May 9, 2017, www.additudemag.com/slideshows/famous -people-with-adhd/.

7   "Can't Stop the (ADHD) Feeling!"

8   Dale Archer, "ADHD: The Entrepreneur's Superpower," *Forbes,* May 14, 2014, www.forbes.com/sites/dalearcher/ 2014/05/14/adhd-the-entrepreneurs-superpower/#74ed0a 3b59e9, adapted.

9   Archer, "ADHD."

10   Archer, *ADHD Advantage,* 112, emphasis added.

11   Archer, "ADHD."

12   Archer, "ADHD."

13   Thom Hartmann, *Attention Deficit Disorder: A Different Perception* (Nevada City, CA: Underwood Books, 1997), as quoted in Archer, *ADHD Advantage,* 71.

14   Archer, *ADHD Advantage,* 70, emphasis added.

Chapter Four

1   Patricia Quinn and Sharon Wigal, "Perceptions of Girls and ADHD: Results from a National Survey," *MedGenMed* 6, no. 2 (2004), www.ncbi.nlm.nih.gov/pmc/articles/PMC 1395774/.

2   "ADD/ADHD," *AmenClinics,* accessed November 17, 2016, www.amenclinics.com/conditions/adhd-add/, adapted.

3   Daniel G. Amen, *Healing ADD: The Breakthrough Program That Allows You to See and Heal the 7 Types of ADD* (New York: Berkley Books, 2013), xv, 91–164.

4   One of the most verified quizzes for self-assessment for ADD has been developed by Dr. Dale Archer and is available in his book *Better than Normal: How What Makes You Different Can Make You Exceptional* (New York: Crown Archetype, 2012), 211.

5   Patricia Quinn in Karen Barrow, "Girl Power(houses): Inspiring Women with ADHD," *ADDitude,* Summer 2011, www.additudemag.com/adhd/article/8642-6.html.

6   See www.apsu.edu/sites/apsu.edu/files/counseling/COGNI TIVE_0.pdf, adapted from David D. Burns, *Feeling Good: The New Mood Therapy* (New York: William Morrow, 1980; Signet, 1981) and David D. Burns, *The Feeling Good Handbook* (New York: Plume, 1999).

Chapter Five

1   "40 Developmental Assets for Adolescents," *Search Institute,* accessed November 30, 2016, www.search-institute .org/content/40-developmental-assets-adolescents-ages -12-18.

2   "Family Strengths," *Search Institute,* accessed November 29, 2016, www.search-institute.org/research/family-strengths.

3   For more on the study, check out the ample resources at www.parentfurther.com.

4   Edward M. Hallowell and John J. Ratey, *Driven to Distrac-
     tion: Recognizing and Coping with Attention Deficit Disor-
     der from Childhood through Adulthood* (New York: Anchor
     Books, 2011), 241–42.

5   "Family Strengths."

6   Melissa Orlov, *The ADHD Effect on Marriage: Understand
     and Rebuild Your Relationship in Six Steps* (Plantation, FL:
     ADD Warehouse, 2010), 5.

7   Orlov, *ADHD Effect on Marriage,* 5–6.

8   Harvard University Resilience Consortium, "Eleven Ivy
     League Universities and Stanford Join as Charter Members
     to Advance Resiliency Research," resilienceconsortium.bsc
     .harvard.edu/.

9   Evernote homepage, https://evernote.com/?var=1.

Chapter Six

1   Daniel G. Amen, *Healing ADD: The Breakthrough Program
     That Allows You to See and Heal the 7 Types of ADD* (New
     York: Berkley Books, 2013), 296.

Chapter Seven

1   See his website at www.jefffoxworthy.com.

2   For a more detailed explanation of the ABCs, check out
     Timothy Smith, *The Danger of Raising Nice Kids: Preparing
     Our Children to Change Their World* (Downers Grove, IL:
     InterVarsity Press, 2006).

3   Edward M. Hallowell and John J. Ratey, *Driven to Distrac-
     tion: Recognizing and Coping with Attention Deficit Disorder*

from Childhood through Adulthood (New York: Anchor Books, 2011), 36.

4   You can explore the homepage at www.trello.com.

5   For more information, see Evernote's homepage, www .evernote.com.

6   A useful instructional video on how to integrate these free apps is "Getting Things Done: Trello, Google Calendar, Evernote, Zapier," YouTube video, posted by "Schurpf," May 20, 2014, www.youtube.com/watch?v=d-6xrvHuLn8.

7   See the five steps here: gettingthingsdone.com/fivesteps/, adapted from David Allen, *Getting Things Done: The Art of Stress-Free Productivity* (New York: Penguin Books, 2015).

8   Allen, *Getting Things Done,* 12.

Chapter Eight

1   Daniel G. Amen, *Healing ADD: The Breakthrough Program That Allows You to See and Heal the 7 Types of ADD* (New York: Berkley Books, 2013), 183.

2   Always discuss with your medical doctor before taking supplements because some supplements and natural remedies will interact with medication. Also for this section, you should know that we aren't on any particular food bandwagon, and we aren't sponsored by the omega-3 fatty acid lobby. However, we do recognize that a nutritious diet and exercise are important (and often neglected) parts of a person's overall health.

3   "6 Essential (and Often-Overlooked) Supplements for ADHD," *ADDitude Magazine,* accessed December 2, 2016, www.additudemag.com/slideshow/29/slide-2.html.

(the building of new neuronal networks), it also offers antiaging properties. We have used EHT for years and have noticed an increase in focus, attention, memory, and brain reserves.

neriumeht.com

www.nerium.com/join/suzannetim

Supplements, Food, Books, Media, and Brain-Healthy Courses

BrainMD

We like the idea of on-demand learning for ADD adults. Learn 24-7 from your smartphone by taking one of these courses.

www.brainmdhealth.com

Websites

Brain Fit Life

Amen Clinics has turned decades of research and clinical experience with patients into fun and motivating science-based games and exercises to help boost your memory, mood, energy, focus, inner peace, sleep, and overall health. *Train your brain—change your life.*

www.mybrainfitlife.com

CDC—Centers for Disease Control and Prevention

How ADHD is diagnosed.

www.cdc.gov/ncbddd/adhd/diagnosis.html

CHADD—Children and Adults with Attention Deficit Disorder

www.chadd.org/Understanding-ADHD/For-Adults.aspx

Amen Clinics

References and Recommended Reading for Healing ADD.
www.amenclinics.com/healingaddreferences

NAMI—National Alliance on Mental Health

Fact sheet on ADHD (PDF).
www.nami.org/NAMI/media/NAMI-Media/Images/FactSheets/
ADHD-FS.pdf

National Institute of Mental Health

Defines ADD/ADHD and lists risk factors and various treatments and therapies. Gives practical tips for organization for
adults. Remember, "There is no cure for ADHD."
www.nimh.nih.gov/health/topics/attention-deficit-hyperactivity
-disorder-adhd/index.shtml

Magazines and Newspapers

ADDitude Magazine

Print and digital, offers well-researched articles for adults with
ADD and those who live with them.
www.additudemag.com

New York Times

A.D.H.D. Seen in 11% of U.S. Children as Diagnoses Rise
www.nytimes.com/2013/04/01/health/more-diagnoses-of
-hyperactivity-causing-concern.html?pagewanted=all&_r=1
Exercising the Mind to Treat Attention Deficits
well.blogs.nytimes.com/2014/05/12/exercising-the-mind
-to-treat-attention-deficits/?rref=collection%2Fbyline

%2Fdaniel-goleman&action=click&contentCollection
= undefined & region = stream & module = stream
_unit&version=latest&contentPlacement=2&pgtype=
collection

Psychology Today

The ADHD Brain: The Quintessential Supercomputer?
www.psychologytoday.com/blog/attention-please/201006/
the-adhd-brain-quintessential-supercomputer

Apps for the ADD'er

Epic Win

Turns tasks into fun quests with a visual countdown timer and
a role playing feature that helps people with ADD enhance
their productivity while having an adventure.
https://itunes.apple.com/us/app/epicwin/id372927221?mt=8

Evernote

Allows you to record, save, write, organize, and search across
devices. Very useful for the ADD brain; especially useful app
for your phone.
https://evernote.com/?var=1

OmniFocus 2

A color-coordinated GUI (graphic user interface) that helps
organize your life and projects. Costs more than Trello but
offers some extra features.
www.omnigroup.com/video/set/omnifocus-2-for-ios/
introducing-omnifocus-2-for-iphone

Trello

An easy-to-use project management app that is visual enough to keep the ADD team members engaged and productive. https://trello.com

Zapier

Allows you to integrate, automate, and innovate by using the application programming to interface between multiple systems, sending and syncing information securely. Connects apps, databases, and services together and syncs them across platforms. https://zapier.com

Events

Annual Conference on ADHD

www.chadd.org/Training-Events/Annual-International -Conference-on-ADHD.aspx

Software

Speech-to-Text Dictation

Dragon Dictation

The premier dictation software to send e-mail, notes, texts, and Twitter updates, useful for all my dictation. Great for busy adults with ADD.

Videos and TED Talks

ADHD: Signs, Symptoms, Research (National Institute of Mental Health)

www.youtube.com/watch?v=IgCL79Jv0lc&feature=youtu.be

Amen Clinics Method Explained by Founder Dr. Daniel Amen

Current medications help fewer people and have a risk of side effects. In this video, Dr. Daniel Amen suggests a better way based on new findings in neuroscience. The Amen Clinic takes a look at the biological, psychological, nutritional, social, and spiritual circles of a patient's life.

www.youtube.com/watch?v=gxgN1cGL5Ao&feature=youtu.be

David Anderson: Your Brain Is More than a Bag of Chemicals

According to Anderson, "Mental illness is caused by disturbances of neural contact versus chemical imbalance of the brain." He presents findings in model organisms.

www.ted.com/talks/david_anderson_your_brain_is_more _than_a_bag_of_chemicals

Theo Siggelakis: Living with ADHD in the Age of Information and Social Media

A recent college grad's entertaining presentation as a *digital native* with ADHD. Siggelakis says, "My brain works like hyperlinks."

www.youtube.com/watch?v=y0hY5TYVv_s

Coaches

ADHD Coaches Organization (ACO)

www.adhdcoaches.org

About New Life Ministries

New Life Ministries, founded by Stephen Arterburn, began in 1988 as New Life Treatment Centers. New Life's nationally broadcast radio program, *New Life Live!*, began in early 1995. The Women of Faith conferences, also founded by Stephen Arterburn, began in 1996. New Life's Counselor Network was formed in 2000, and TV.NewLife.com, the ministry's Internet-based television channel, was launched in 2014. New Life continues to develop and expand their programs and resources to help meet the changing needs of their callers and listeners.

Today, New Life Ministries is a nationally recognized, faith-based broadcasting and counseling nonprofit organization that provides ministry through radio, TV, their counseling network, workshops, and support groups, as well as through their numerous print, audio, and video resources. All New Life resources are based on God's truth and help those who are hurting find and build connections and experience life transformation.

The *New Life Live!* radio program, still the centerpiece of the ministry, is broadcast on Christian radio stations in more than 150 markets. It can also be seen on several network and online channels.

New Life's mission is to reach out compassionately to those seeking emotional and spiritual health and healing for God's glory. New Life Ministries Resource Center receives thousands of calls each month from those looking for help.

For more information, visit newlife.com.

NEWLIFE

Help in Life's Hardest Places

Talking about the things no one else will, to bring healing to those who've lost hope

"I have been living with my secrets for 30 plus years while failing time and again to stop and all the while them getting worse. For the first time I have learned more about why it is happening, developing an action plan to change, and creating a network of support."

— *Jack*
Intensive Workshop attendee

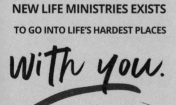
When you or someone you love is in crisis, you need a trusted friend to walk alongside you—a helper who's been there and understands, but who also has the training and skill to offer practical help.

New Life Ministries, founded by Steve Arterburn, exists to go into life's hardest places with you.

For over 30 years, we've provided expert answers to people just like you on our call-in radio show, *New Life Live!* We also offer a host of other resources, Intensive Workshops, and referrals to a carefully selected network of counselors.

Visit NewLife.com today to see how we can help, or call 800-HELP-4-ME. We want to hear from you!

About Stephen Arterburn

Stephen Arterburn, M.Ed., is the founder and chairman of New Life Ministries and host of the number-one nationally syndicated Christian counseling talk show *New Life Live!*, heard and watched by more than two million people each week on nearly two hundred stations nationwide. He is also the host of *New Life TV*, a web-based channel dedicated to transforming lives through God's truth, and he also serves as a teaching pastor in Indianapolis, Indiana.

Stephen is an internationally recognized public speaker and has been featured on national media venues such as *Oprah*, *Inside Edition*, *Good Morning America*, *CNN Live*, and *ABC World News Tonight*; in the *New York Times*, *USA Today*, *US News and World Report*; and even in *GQ* and *Rolling Stone* magazines. Stephen has spoken at major events for the National Center for Fathering, American Association of Christian Counselors, Promise Keepers Canada, the Lifewell Conference in Australia, and the Salvation Army, to name a few.

He is the bestselling author of books such as *Every Man's Battle* and *Healing Is a Choice*. With more than eight million books in print, Stephen has been writing about God's transformational truth since 1984. His ministry focuses on identifying and compassionately responding to the needs of those seeking healing and restoration through God's truth. Along with Dr. Dave Stoop, he edited and produced the number-one-bestselling *Life Recovery Bible*.

Stephen has degrees from Baylor University and the University of North Texas, as well as two honorary doctorates, and is currently completing his doctoral studies in Christian counseling. He resides with his family in Fishers, Indiana. Stephen Arterburn can be contacted directly at SArterburn@newlife.com.

About Timothy Smith

Timothy Smith, M.Ed., is a family coach, author, and speaker. He is a national leader in family ministry and is committed to helping people grow healthy families and marriages.

With thirty years' experience in working with children, youth, and families, and with degrees in psychology and educational psychology (M.A., Biola University) and postgraduate work and research in the fields of positive psychology and coaching, Tim cofounded and leads Life Skills for American Families, a nonprofit organization dedicated to innovatively celebrating and empowering the family. Visit www .parentscoach.org for more information. Tim is also a research fellow with the George H. Gallup International Institute of Princeton.

Tim's popular book *The Seven Cries of Today's Teens* is based on exclusive data from Gallup. His recent books and seminars include *52 Creative Family Time Experiences, Simple Solutions for Families in the Fast Lane,* and his bestseller *The Danger of Raising Nice Kids. Understanding and Loving a Person with Attention Deficit Disorder* is his twenty-first book.

Tim is probably best known for his humorous and practical presentations to thousands of parents, married couples, and men each year. His speaking clients include the Young Presidents' Organization, the National Football League, Clear Channel Communications, the Cleveland Clinic, Pepperdine University, and other nationally recognized corporations and institutions, including numerous churches and schools.

In his free time, he enjoys surfing. He has been married to his wife, Suzanne, for thirty-plus years, and they live in California. They have two married daughters and two grandsons.